Darlene Sala

REFRESHING WORDS
WORDS
for
BUSY
WOMEN

HARVEST HOUSE PUBLISHERS

EUGENE, OREGON

Cover photo © Collage Photography / Veer

Backcover author photo by Jeff Vasquez

Cover design by e210 Design, Egan, Minnesota

REFRESHING WORDS FOR BUSY WOMEN
Copyright © 2010 by Darlene Sala
Published by Harvest House Publishers
Eugene, Oregon 97402
www.harvesthousepublishers.com

ISBN 978-0-7369-2613-3

Printed in China

10 11 12 13 14 15 16 17 18 / RDS-SK / 10 9 8 7 6 5 4 3 2 1

*Dedicated to all busy women who need
a breath of invigorating, revitalizing,
restorative, health-giving, fresh air.*

*May God use these thoughts to energize
you and renew your focus on the Lord,
who wants to direct your busy life.*

In Appreciation

I thank God for the prayers and encouragement of the able staff at Harvest House Publishers, including the accomplished editing skills of Barbara Gordon.

A very special thank you for revision help goes to my eldest daughter, Bonnie Craddick. (You'll write your own book some day, Bonnie.)

Also, I want to mention Harold, my husband. His patience was exceptional. It's not always fun being around someone who is buried in writing. The redeeming factor was that he was writing a book at the same time!

Dear Reader . . .

Life for women on the go is draining, sometimes suffocating. All the more important, then, to stop and *breathe*. And the written word can help. I like the way author Philip Yancey put it: "I saw that writing could penetrate into the crevices, bringing spiritual oxygen to people trapped in airtight boxes."[1] Bringing this vital spiritual oxygen to busy women is exactly the purpose of this book.

These short, easy-to-read selections will refresh, strengthen, and sometimes challenge you. Because they are Scripture based and always encouraging, I hope they will give you a breath of fresh air every day and provide special rejuvenation when life has you gasping.

I will refresh the weary and satisfy the faint.
JEREMIAH 31:25

Darlene Sala

All of Me

A pastor tells about the time his young son burst into his office after the morning session at the church's preschool.

"Here, Dad, this is for you," the boy said as he thrust a sheet of photographs into his hand. It was the typical pane of a dozen identical student photos—enough for every relative in the family.

"These are great, Son," his dad responded, reaching for the scissors so he could snip one off to keep.

"No, Dad." His son stopped him. "Don't cut them. I want you to have *all* of me."

How like our heavenly Father, thought the pastor as he slipped the sheet of photos under the glass that covered his desk. *How He must long for us to run into His presence and declare, "I want you to have all of me!" Not offering him 10 percent, or one day a week, or some of our abilities. But because we love Him so much, throwing ourselves into His arms just as a little child does.*

Hymn writer Frances Ridley Havergal penned these words:

Take my love; my Lord,
I pour at Thy feet its treasure store;
take my self, and I will be ever,
only, all for thee.[2]

Today we might not express it so formally, but that's the kind of outpouring of love that brings joy to our heavenly Father's heart. The psalmist wrote, "I will praise you, O LORD, with *all* my heart...I seek you with all my heart" (Psalm 9:1 and 119:10). Let your commitment to the Lord be the spontaneous expression of your heart, holding nothing back.

Spiritual Oxygen

The flight attendant recited the usual instructions. "If loss of cabin pressure should occur, oxygen masks will drop down. If you are traveling with a child, secure your own mask *before* putting the mask on your child." That seems counterintuitive to moms because we're used to putting our children first. However, the attendant explained, "If *you* should black out from lack of oxygen, you wouldn't be able to help your child. It makes sense to put your own mask on first."

And something similar occurs when we're parenting. We mothers usually feel we must always tend to our children's needs before our own, and sometimes we're pretty close to blacking out from exhaustion! And especially when it comes to spiritual resources, moms often come up short. When I was mothering three young children, there simply wasn't time for extensive Bible study or long blocks of time dedicated to prayer. The best I could do was grab a few verses on the run and send up prayers of desperation, saying, "Lord, please help me!"

So my advice to moms? Don't panic when a few days

go by and you haven't completed a Bible study or you've had to keep your prayers very short. Reading a short psalm as you brew the morning coffee, praising God as you look into your baby's face during a diaper change, or perhaps listening to scripture CDs as you drive car pool may be all you can manage right now. And it will do until you have more time. Every little bit will help!

The same principle is true whether you're responsible for children or all the employees at a large corporation. You can't go very long without spiritual oxygen. Jesus said, "Man does not live on bread alone, but on every word that comes from the mouth of God" (Matthew 4:4). Several small meals a day have been shown to be very healthy! Make sure you keep nibbling throughout the day when a sit-down dinner isn't possible.

The Power of Presence

While visiting the ancient city of Petra in Jordan, one of our group felt faint and needed to lie down. I stayed with her as the others continued to explore the area. Soon a cluster of local men politely sat near us to communicate their concern, although they didn't say a word. That's the power of presence.

This took my thoughts to the book of Job, and Job's days of suffering. When he lost his wealth, his children, and his health, three of his friends came to comfort him. "They sat on the ground with him for seven days and seven nights. No one said a word to him, because they saw how great his suffering was" (Job 2:13). That too is the power of presence. In fact, when his friends began to talk they caused him more discomfort than help.

Kay Warren says that as she was going through breast cancer, she found the greatest comfort...

> not in the verses of Scripture people sent me or the
> fantastic meals prepared by loving church members
> or the books on living with cancer. What comforted

me was the *presence* of family members and friends who were willing to sit with me, sometimes without saying a single word. They brought the supernatural comfort of the Holy Spirit to my suffering just by *being with me.*[3]

When people we care about suffer tragedies in their lives, we are sometimes hesitant to visit them because we don't know what to say. As God's children, He lives within us, so let's not hesitate to spend time with those who suffer, knowing that when we do, we are taking the presence of Christ to them—even without speaking a word.

A Gift for God

Before the temple was built in Jerusalem, the people of Israel met in a portable "Tent of Meeting." Inside was an altar for sacrifices, as well as other articles, including a bronze washbasin for the priests. God instructed Moses that whenever the priests entered the Tent of Meeting to offer sacrifices, they were to first wash their hands and feet with water from the bronze basin.

At the time that the Tent was constructed, God's people were in a wilderness area, and bronze wasn't available at a local hardware store. So where did they get it? The Bible says they made the basin "from the mirrors of the women who served at the entrance to the Tent of Meeting" (Exodus 38:8). We don't know what those women's responsibilities actually were, but the "serve" tells us that their hearts were devoted to God.

Women used polished plates of brass for mirrors because polished glass hadn't been invented yet. Just like us, they cared about their appearance enough to carry these with them as they moved from place to place. But when their precious mirrors were needed for God's purpose, they willingly gave them up.

There's nothing wrong with caring about how you look. I believe we honor God when we maintain an attractive appearance. But the hearts of these women were touched with the need for God's meeting place so deeply that they were willing to give up one of their most treasured possessions for Him.

Which is more important to you? How you look or what God wants? This is a matter of the heart.

Always on the Job

Dorothy Nicholas and her husband were talking to their next-door neighbors, a young couple who had helped them on many occasions. Almost out of the blue, one of the neighbors began to tell them of his difficult past. As a teen growing up in small town in South Carolina, he'd become involved with the wrong crowd and ended up spending a year in a reformatory. When he was released, he had problems finding a job.

In desperation he decided to rob a gas station to get enough money to leave the state. He stole his father's car and gun and drove to a local station just before closing time. He was about to demand all the money from the woman manager when he looked up and saw a sign over the service window that read, "God Is Our Security Guard—Always on the Job." Suddenly he realized he couldn't rob that place. Guilt-laden, he rushed home and prayed all night, asking for forgiveness and the courage to live right. And with God's help, he did.

Hearing the story, Dorothy looked at her husband. Both were thinking of a night 13 years earlier in a small town in

South Carolina. They were working on ideas for a sign for their business. Finally the right words came. The slogan Dorothy's husband put on the sign at the small gas station they managed was "God Is Our Security Guard—Always on the Job."[4]

Yes, truly God was "on the job"...and He always will be. Psalm 121 says, "He will not let your foot slip—he who watches over you will not slumber" (Psalm 121:3). Your greatest security rests in Him.

The Pain of the Past

Too many people who have been wronged have "built a memorial to the event and placed it smack dab in the center of the living room of their lives, going there every day to worship," so says a retired minister.[5] A memorial to a wrong done in the past. I'd never thought of it that way, but I think he's right.

A man came to my husband for counsel, bringing with him a file about three inches thick. Years ago someone had wronged him, and ever since he'd been collecting evidence of the injustice. Every day he visited his "memorial" to this hurtful event.

Memories can be tremendous blessings as we recall happy days from the past. But memories can also be tremendously painful. Why do we tend to pull up wounding events from the past and relive them over and over and over again? When we do this, we're not being survivors; we're being perpetual victims.

Why not break down any monuments you've erected to the past? You can't erase it from your memory, of course, but you can refuse to make it a worship center. Instead, each time that painful memory comes to mind, bring it to the Lord and dump it on Him. God doesn't mind. In fact, He says, "Forget the former things; do not dwell on the past" (Isaiah 43:18).

Today is the only day we really have. Yesterday is gone, and whether we get a tomorrow is unknown. Honor God today by leaving the past with Him.

The Right Place,
the Right Time

In 1949, when Billy Graham held his first big tent revival in Los Angeles, some of Hollywood's most famous people accepted Christ. Among those was Jim Voss, an electronics genius who was a wire-tapper for gangster Mickey Cohen. After the meetings ended, Billy asked Jim if he would come to Boston and give his testimony in the Boston Garden, which seated over 14,000. Jim was eager to participate, but when he looked at his date book, he discovered he'd already committed those days to a little church in the heart of southeast Los Angeles. Jim kept his word and spoke at the small church.

One evening after one of the meetings, FBI agents met him. "You're under arrest for your part in the Brinks Robbery," they said. At that time the robbery in Boston was the largest heist in the history of the United States—the "crime of the century." The stolen cash alone amounted to $1.2 billion.

"Well," Jim told them, "I wasn't *in* Boston."

When the case came to court, Jim had a couple hundred people who could testify he was in their church every night during the time just before, during, and after the robbery. The FBI told him that had he gone to Boston, there is no way he could have proven he didn't take part in it because of his extensive criminal history.

Jim learned that God truly does direct our steps. Psalm 43:3 says, "Send forth your light and your truth, let them guide me." God's light directs us—not as a dazzling spotlight that illuminates the whole horizon of our future, but as a flashlight that gives us just enough light for the next step.

"Send Me!"

The prophet Isaiah had a most unusual vision of heaven. He saw the Lord seated on a throne and heard Him ask, "Whom shall I send? And who will go for us?" God had a message He wanted conveyed to His people on earth. Quickly Isaiah responded, "Here am I. Send me!" (Isaiah 6:8). So God used him to carry His words to the people.

Christian author and speaker Jill Briscoe wrote a book she humorously titled *Here Am I—Send Aaron*. She was referring to the experience Moses had when God called him to lead His people out of Egypt and into the land He'd promised them. Unlike Isaiah, Moses dug in his heels and made excuses, essentially saying, "Who am I, that I should go? What should I tell the people? What if they don't believe me? I'm not eloquent. O Lord, please send someone else." Eventually, in anger, God told him to take his brother, Aaron, to be his mouthpiece (Exodus 3–4).

Don't be too hard on Moses though. Under the same circumstances, we too might have responded, "Here am I, Lord...but send someone else." Moses had run from Egypt 40 years earlier because he was wanted for murder. He had no idea what would happen if he again set foot on Egyptian soil.

We know the end of the story now. God used Moses in a mighty way to deliver His people from slavery.

What is God asking you to do? Perhaps something that seems far beyond your abilities? If He calls you, He will also enable you. So when you hear His voice, respond by saying, "Here am I, Lord. Send me!"

The Comfort of Hope

I attended my grandson's high school graduation. The diplomas were presented to the seniors by their parents. Since this was a homeschool group, emotions ran high as each set of parents spoke a few words expressing heart-deep thoughts to their children. These parents had not only nurtured them but spent countless hours educating them as well.

I was impressed that every senior was accompanied to the microphone by two parents—so unusual in today's world of broken families. All, that is, except Kristen. Her mom, Carol, would so much have wanted to be there for this moment. But her life had been cruelly taken three years earlier by a man who went on a rampage, pistol-whipping three members of the family. Kristen's two siblings survived, but their mom did not. Kristen's dad presented the diploma to his daughter alone.

The family tragedy seemed senseless. Why had God not prevented the trauma? The reality of life is that hard things happen to believers and unbelievers alike. The difference is that we who have faith in Jesus Christ are not without hope, for we'll be with our loved one again in heaven. To go through a tragedy without that hope is to despair. To go through the same situation with the Lord is to have assurance that brings comfort the unbeliever does not have.

> In a flash, in the twinkling of an eye, at the last trumpet...the dead will be raised imperishable...and we will be changed (1 Corinthians 15:52).

Kristen's family is awaiting that glorious family reunion.

Abandoned? Never Again!

D id you grow up in a one-parent home? Maybe your father deserted your mother so your home was torn apart. You may not think you're worth very much because if you were, your dad wouldn't have left. The sense of abandonment you feel may present another problem: You may have difficulty thinking of God as your loving heavenly Father.

A friend of mine says that the only thing that helped her with that concept was studying the characteristics of "God as Father" in the Bible. Instead of using her experiences with her earthly father to help her understand God, she did the reverse—learned what kind of a father God is and then told herself, "That's the way a human father should be."

The least likely people in the world to abandon you are your parents. A mother will usually believe in her child even when everyone else gives up. Yet Psalm 27:10 says, "Though my father and mother forsake me, the LORD will receive me." In Psalm 9:10, David said, "You, LORD, have never forsaken those who seek you." The word "forsake" isn't one we use frequently nowadays, but think of its synonyms: "abandon," "desert," "leave," "disown," "relinquish," "give up." These describe what God will *never* do to you. On the contrary, when you become God's child, He puts His Spirit within you so He literally never leaves you!

God has taken you into His family. He is your Father, and you can count on Him.

Satisfied

For a long time now I've been fascinated with the second verse in Psalm 131: "I have stilled and quieted my soul; like a weaned child with its mother, like a weaned child is my soul within me." My three children as tiny babies were eager—almost frantic—to be near me when they were hungry. But by the time they were two years old, they would sit quietly on my lap because they were weaned and used to being fed in a high chair.

Many of us are like needy newborn babies. Every time we pray, we want something from God. Of course He doesn't mind, but I can't help thinking He would be pleased if sometimes we came into His presence just for the joy of closeness with Him.

Can you relate to the desire to have someone with you? Wawa Ponce wanted a husband. She was sad that God hadn't yet satisfied her yearning to have someone special to share her life with. Her deep longing was almost a physical pain. Then God led her to this verse in Psalm 131. Reflecting on the image of the young child peacefully cradled in her mother's arms so quiet, so still, she wrote,

I want to be that child. No, I need to be that child. I
need God to wean me from what I want, to prepare
me for what He wants for me. I need to be still in His
arms knowing that He would take care of my needs—
even my wants.[6]

Then she concluded with a prayer of acceptance: "Lord,
I will wait and be satisfied with Your answer." And peace
came.

Have you quieted your soul? You can find peace in
God's arms.

A Brand-New Beginning

Is your past keeping you from being your best right now? Past sins can do that, you know. David Eckman wrote,

> Sin walks us into a huge warehouse filled with video clips of us and says, "This is your life. We have thousands of clips of your failures. Many of them are so embarrassing that you wouldn't want to show them to your children. That is all you are, and we have the record of it. So you might as well surrender to sin within, because you can't be better than this. You are these clips—and nothing else."

Perhaps you're convinced your past is who you are and nothing can change that. There's good news! "Jesus has burned the warehouse!"[7] The Bible tells us,

> We know that our old self was crucified with him so that the body of sin might be done away with, that we should no longer be slaves to sin—because anyone who has died has been freed from sin...In the same way, count yourselves dead to sin but alive to God in Christ Jesus (Romans 6:6-7,11).

Those video clips are a true picture of your past, no doubt about it. But Jesus paid the penalty that justice demands for your wrongs. When you accept God's forgiveness, it's as if you died and rose again to a new life. And that's where God wants you to live—in the present, not the past. As a Christian, you are not the sum of your past. You are a brand-new person with a brand-new beginning.

Questioning or Trusting?

When life throws circumstances at us we can't understand, we either question God or trust Him. Lisa Beamer learned that lesson—twice.

Lisa is the wife of September 11 (2001) hero Todd Beamer, who, with other passengers on United Airlines Flight 93, wrestled control from hijackers long enough that the plane crashed instead of being used as a weapon against the White House.

After the crash, while dealing with her husband's death, Lisa's mind drifted back to when her father had died quite suddenly when she was 15. At that time she'd wrestled with God, saying, "God, You could have prevented this if You had wanted to! Why didn't You?" Then one day a college administrator asked her if it was time to accept that, for whatever reason, God had allowed his death to happen.[8] After that, Bible verses Lisa had recently read came to mind:

> Oh, the depth of the riches of the wisdom and
>   knowledge of God!
> How unsearchable his judgments,
>   and his paths beyond tracing out!

"Who has known the mind of the Lord?
  Or who has been his counselor?"

"Who has ever given to God,
  that God should repay him?"

For from him and through him and to him are all
    things.
To him be the glory forever! Amen

(Romans 11:33-36).

Lisa had finally decided, "Who am I to question God? I think I deserve a happy life so I get angry when it doesn't always happen." Then she made a conscious decision to stop questioning and start trusting.

And now, so many years later, she had to lean on that decision again as she dealt with the tragedy of Todd's death.

No, we don't—and can't—understand all that happens in this life. But we can decide to trust God and receive His peace in every painful situation.

A Sensitive Heart

Sometimes we're so busy that we don't hear God's quiet voice telling us about something special He has for us to do, such as offer a loving touch, comforting words, even a short prayer with someone who is hurting.

Freda Robinson is one of my heroes for the outstanding work she does among the poor of Kitale, Kenya. She's a wonderful example of someone who takes time to care for people. Early in her career, before she had her own hospital and outreach, she was the head nurse at the best private hospital in the city. One day Sister Freda finished her work and went home. But as soon as she entered the doorway she felt an unmistakable urge to return to the hospital. Not able to brush it aside, she turned and went back.

Reentering the hospital, Sister Freda strode down the hallway. Passing by the prenatal care ward, she peeked in at the babies because children have always been a soft spot in her heart. Suddenly she stopped. One baby caught her well-trained eye. The little boy didn't appear to be breathing. Rushing to the incubator, she snatched him up and began to massage his chest and resuscitate him.

"I felt the guiding hand of God that day," recalls Sister Freda. "As I worked with him, he gasped once. I gave him oxygen and he began to breathe normally. Today Mr. Korir is an attorney in Kitale."

Galatians 5:25 says, "Since we live by the Spirit, let us keep in step with the Spirit." May God help us always be sensitive and responsive to His gentle voice.

The Snake Is Dead

Pastor Glenn Burris likes to share about a time when he hauled their large garbage containers out to the street for pickup—and the simple task took on an unexpected twist.

> I had just rolled out the third can when I noticed… the snake. It was about five or six feet long and was lying in some grass just off our driveway. My heart was racing as I grabbed my cell phone and called [my wife] Debbie, who was inside the house…I didn't want to leave in case the snake crawled away because then I would worry about where it might go.
>
> When Debbie answered her phone, I quickly got to the point: "Grab the shovel and meet me at the street near the driveway. There's a humongous snake in our yard!"
>
> Her response was much too calm. "I'll be glad to bring the shovel, but the snake is already dead," she said. "The gardener…killed it and left it in the yard for the crows to take."

In just about 15 seconds, my whole perspective changed. The source of fear that had gripped me so strongly just minutes before was now easily explained.[9]

The purpose of the story? What we fear often never takes place. Like Pastor Glenn, we often worry about "dead snakes."

Because God knows fear is a natural human reaction, over and over again in the Bible He tells us, "Do not be afraid." He illustrates this principle with people who thought they were going to starve, drown, be killed in war, die in childbirth, or be murdered. But in their seemingly scary circumstances, God brought them through unscathed. So before you panic about a situation, look again. The snake may not even be alive.

When God Speaks

John's phone rang. His teenage daughter was involved in an accident. Would he come? A short time later he was sitting on a curb with his daughter waiting for the police to write up a report on the accident, which, fortunately, had wrecked the car but caused no human injuries. All at once John began to seethe inside. Why hadn't his daughter been more careful? Didn't she realize how serious this could have been? The more he thought about it, the angrier he became.

Then something caught his attention...a piece of paper floating in the gutter. As he looked more closely, he saw it was the fill-in-the-blanks outline from Sunday's sermon at his church. The title of the message had been "Defusing Your Anger." Getting up and walking over, he picked it up. He had to smile as he realized how creative God can be in getting His people's attention.

Yes, God speaks to us in many ways. Sometimes as we read the Bible, sometimes through a scripture we memorized years ago, sometimes through a friend's biblical advice. Other times God speaks in our hearts with a quiet but insistent voice. If He needs to, He can even float His message to us in the gutter.

"Are you listening for God?"

God once said to His people, "I spoke to you again and again, but you did not listen; I called you, but you did not answer" (Jeremiah 7:13). How sad! James wrote, "Everyone should be quick to listen, slow to speak and slow to become angry" (James 1:19). Then he added, "Do not merely listen to the word...Do what it says" (verse 22). Good counsel, James!

Farther Than You Can See

I used to look forward each month to turning to the last page in my mother's *Better Homes and Gardens* magazine to read a column that Bill Vaughan wrote under the pen name Burton Hillis. In one of his witty observations of everyday life, he gave insights into his own boyhood:

> "It is only a little farther," my father used to say when I was a little boy, winded and leg weary, out on the long Sunday afternoon walks that we used to take together. So I would brace up and struggle on a little longer, looking for the first familiar landmarks that would indicate we were back in our own neighborhood.

Then one day Burton asked his father how far "a little farther" really was. "It is farther than you can see," he replied, "but not as far as you can go."[10]

Like the walks Burton's father planned, the destinations God sets before us are often beyond our sight. We can't see over the ridge or around the bend, nor do we know how much further we have to go before we reach home. But Isaiah assures us, "Whether you turn to the right or to the left, your ears will hear a voice behind you, saying, 'This is the way; walk in it'" (Isaiah 30:21). He also says, "Those who hope in the LORD…will walk and not be faint" (40:31).

Perhaps the goal you've been working toward seems a long way off, and you wonder if you will *ever* get there. Keep going a little farther—perhaps farther than you can see, but not as far as you can go if you keep your hand in God's.

Dorcas Had a Needle

She lived in Joppa, on the edge of the sparkling Mediterranean. Day after day she picked up her needle to create coats and garments she envisioned in her mind. Dorcas "was always doing good and helping the poor" (Acts 9:36). We don't know if she made clothing for the poor or sold her handiwork to help them, but we do know she was called a "disciple." And probably she was a widow, for when she died, the widows in her neighborhood or town came to mourn. They knew Dorcas would be terribly missed.

The apostle Peter was sent for, and he came. Through Peter, God miraculously raised Dorcas back to life to continue her sewing ministry! "This became known all over Joppa, and many people believed in the Lord" (Acts 9:42).

Dorcas had a needle, and she used it for God's glory.

You may be a klutz when it comes to sewing…but you may be excellent at bookkeeping. Use your pencil for God. Maybe you don't know what to do with an artist's brush, but you are a wonderful cook. Use your spatula for God. Perhaps you could never be a nurse because you can't stand the sight of blood. But if given a few flowers and a bit of greenery, you can create a lovely arrangement. Use your floral skills for Him.

Whether it's a camera, a pen, a gardening trowel, or something else, use it to bless God and help the needy people around you. Dorcas would tell you that you'll find far more joy than you would ever have using your skills only for yourself.

Single Again

"Single after 60 good years of marriage" is not a stage of life wives want to think about. That's why I asked two women going through this uncharted period of their lives to share their thoughts.

Michelle told me, "We really had a good marriage with a lot of fun packed into it. I miss having someone to talk to and to make decisions with."

Victoria wrote, "No one can take the place of your best friend and lover. At night you especially feel the reality of death and your own fragile vulnerability to it. Friendships also change. Some people don't call because they don't know what to say."

"It gets somewhat easier with time," Michelle observed. "Someone told me that grief is like powerful ocean waves that pound the shore. As time goes by, the waves don't come with such regularity, but when they do come they are just as intense."

God wants to be our all every day of our lives, regardless of the life stage we're in: single, married, or single again. The apostle Paul said that "the widow who is...left all alone puts her hope in God and continues night and day to pray and to ask God for help" (1 Timothy 5:5).

Actually that's what all of us should do! Author Eugenia Price wrote, "We limit [God] when we think of his being in charge of the death [of a loved one] only. God is also in charge of the one who is left behind."[11] Why not ask God how He wants you to serve Him at this stage in your life?

A True Heart for Christ

Bill wore a T-shirt with holes in it, jeans, and flip-flops—his wardrobe for his entire four years of college. Admittedly a bit strange though very bright, Bill had become a Christian while attending college.

Across the street from the campus was a very conservative church where people dressed up to attend. They wanted to develop a ministry to students but weren't sure how to go about it.

One day Bill decided to attend. He wore his usual attire. When he entered the packed church, people watched a bit uncomfortably as he proceeded down the aisle and, not finding a seat, finally sat down right on the carpet at the front. The tension in the air was thick.

Then the minister noticed that from the back of the church a deacon was slowly making his way toward Bill. The godly, silver-haired gentleman in his eighties was wearing a fine suit—very elegant, very dignified. Everyone was thinking, *You can't blame him. How can you expect a man of his age and background to understand some college kid on the floor?*

When the elderly man made it to the front, with great difficulty he lowered himself to the floor and sat down next to Bill so he wouldn't be alone.

Softly the minister began, "What I'm about to preach, you will never remember. What you have just seen, you will never forget. My sermon text this morning is Ephesians 5:15: 'Be very careful, then, how you live—not as unwise but as wise.'" And then he added, "You may be the only Bible some people will ever read."

Living at High Speed

A fighter pilot flying upside down at tremendous speed became disoriented and pulled the flight stick in the wrong direction. A few moments later flaming wreckage was all that remained. Commenting on this tragedy, writer Del Fehsenfeld pointed out that most of us are in danger of making the same mistake—traveling so fast in life that we become mixed up about what is most important. He observed,

> Disorientation at a high rate of speed is a deadly combination for all of us. Capacity for discernment is diminished…The result is a high risk of careening in wrong directions.

For many of us, living at full throttle is our normal way of life. What we need is a pause in our activities that makes "room to listen and linger. Room to receive and reorient. Room to 'be still and know' that there is a God—and we aren't Him!"[12] We live as if we, not God, are the ones who make things happen in life. We work as if everything depends on us. Consequently, most of us, as Fehsenfeld puts it, are "running on physical, emotional and spiritual fumes."

How do we get our lives back in balance again? "Come to me," Jesus said simply (Matthew 11:28). The reality is that when most of us come to the Lord, we want to do all the talking rather than listen to Him.

If your life has become a racetrack of activity, stop. Find a quiet space and talk to God. Tell Him, "Lord, I give up. I'm coming to You to realign my priorities and refill my fuel tank." Then listen.

A Life Preserver

D avid was born with a premature nervous system. Everything over-stimulated him, especially touch. He had no ability to calm himself, so he cried day and night, sleeping for only 20 minutes at a time. Terri, his mom, recalls those exhausting months:

> We could not touch his feet, head, or hands because this is where the nerve endings are, and the slightest touch would cause him excruciating pain.

> His doctor told me to get help because I could possibly go psychotic and hurt my baby due to lack of sleep. On top of that he warned that 70 percent of marriages with children like this end in divorce. Then he said to hang in there—that it would take "only" two years for my son's nervous system to be completely normal.

Terri wasn't sure she would live that long! Amazingly, Bill and Terri's marriage survived and in fact became stronger. "We gave each other grace for misspoken words and misunderstandings," Terri recalls. Bill stepped down from his corporate job to spend more time with his family.

Perhaps no couple ever held on so doggedly to Philippians 4:13: "I can do all things through Him [Christ] who strengthens me" (NASB). These words were a life preserver to which they clung in desperation.

Today David is a perfectly normal teen who loves the Lord and excels. "I would never wish to go through that again," Terri adds, "but I'm grateful the Lord used my son's physical problem to mature my relationship with Him and with my husband."

In your impossible situation, hold on to Christ. Terri would assure you that "only He can give you strength to go on."

Where Is God?

When we pray, sometimes we sense God's presence right there with us. Other times God seems very far away. Somebody quipped, "If God seems far away, guess who moved!" But I don't think that is necessarily true. That would be tantamount to asserting that if you can't "feel" God's presence, He must not be there. Feelings *follow* faith; they don't precede it.

Moses declared that God is *always* near when we pray: "What other nation is so great as to have their gods near them the way the LORD our God is near us whenever we pray to him?" (Deuteronomy 4:7).

The size of space can sometimes make it seem like God is far away since the universe is so vast. We may think that because He's beyond all that comprises our universe, He must be...or can be...a great distance from where we are. Don't believe it for a moment! Our God is big enough to be everywhere at the same time. When David tried to think of a place where God is not, he gave up:

Where can I go from your Spirit?
Where can I flee from your presence?

If I go up to the heavens, you are there;
if I make my bed in the depths, you are there.

If I rise on the wings of the dawn,
if I settle on the far side of the sea,

even there your hand will guide me,
your right hand will hold me fast

(Psalm 139:7-10).

So when you pray, don't trust your feelings about whether God is listening. As Moses said, "The LORD our God is near us whenever we pray." He's listening to every word!

Chocolate Cake

As people walked into church that Sunday morning, they saw a small table next to the pulpit. On it were some small food cartons, a bowl, a measuring cup, and a large spoon. What was all this doing in church?

As my dad began his sermon, he first held up the measuring cup and a package of flour. As he poured the flour into the cup he asked, "Who would volunteer to come up here and eat these two cups of flour?" No one responded. He teased them a little. "Why, everyone knows that many delicious things contain flour. This is the best flour. Someone come." Still no one responded.

Then he poured cocoa into the cup. "Well, will someone come and eat this good cocoa?" Again no volunteers—not even the children.

Next he offered shortening. No takers.

"How about a couple teaspoons of vanilla?" Still no response.

His text for the morning's sermon was Romans 8:28: "We know that in all things God works for the good of those who love him, who have been called according to his purpose." The application was plain. Often things happen to us in life which, when viewed by themselves, don't make sense—and sometimes don't even taste very good. But when mixed together—well, just wait!

At this point my mom walked onto the platform carrying a scrumptious-looking chocolate cake. Delicious! Needless to say, there were plenty of takers for that!

Don't focus on the negative incidents in your life. If you are God's child, you can be sure He will work them together with the surrounding circumstances for your good. God knows how to make wonderful chocolate cake!

If Only . . .

A young woman in her twenties commented to me that she really has no choice but to obey God because when she doesn't, she is the loser. At a young age she had figured out the very important principle that God's will, as difficult as it may sometimes be, is always the best.

God longs to bring good into our lives. In the Old Testament book of Isaiah we read,

> This is what the LORD says—
> your Redeemer, the Holy One of Israel:
>
> "I am the LORD your God,
> who teaches you what is best for you,
> who directs you in the way you should go.
>
> If only you had paid attention to my commands,
> your peace would have been like a river,
> your righteousness like the waves of the sea"
>
> (Isaiah 48:17-18).

"If only..." God says. If only you had waited a little longer before marrying that guy who doesn't share your faith... If only you had pursued God's will for your life when you still had a chance to choose the direction your life would go... If only you had shown more patience and tenderness toward your kids while they were still living at home.

Well, you can't go back and unscramble scrambled eggs. What's done is done. But you can make a decision that from this point on you will obey God and choose to do His will. And He will help you!

Remember that He is the Lord your God, who "teaches you what is best for you, who directs you in the way you should go." Look to Him for guidance. Obey Him and find peace.

Taming Your Tongue

Sue Augustine writes, "I had to chuckle when I read what Elisabeth Elliot said about our words: 'Never pass up an opportunity to keep your mouth shut!'" Then Sue continues,

> Over the years, I have learned to pray, "Lord, walk beside me with one hand on my shoulder and the other over my mouth!" On days when my emotions threaten to rage out of control, my family members often overhear my hollering. "Oh, Lord—please shut my mouth before I say what's on my mind!"[13]

Can you relate? Scripture says, "We all stumble in many ways. If anyone is never at fault in what he says, he is a perfect man, able to keep his whole body in check" (James 3:2).

I have yet to meet that perfect person who never says something she shouldn't. That's why we need Holy Spirit control in our lives. Many sermons are preached on the fruit of the Holy Spirit listed in Galatians 5:22-23: "love, joy, peace, patience, kindness, goodness, faithfulness, gentleness and self-control." The preacher gives instructions for producing each of these qualities as if they are separate "fruits" that we can grow in our lives. But I believe they are nine descriptions of one work God's Spirit will do in our lives if we let Him be in charge.

Controlling what you say seems to be one of the last characteristics to be evident because it's so difficult to master. In fact, as James 3:8 says, "No man can tame the tongue." Only God can help you take on your tongue. Proverbs 25:28 says, "Like a city whose walls are broken down is a man who lacks self-control." When you ask God's Spirit to be in charge of all of your life, He will help you control what you say.

When Your Hut's on Fire

When it comes to God's work in our lives, an often-told illustration captures His awesome provision:

The disheveled man had been washed up on a small, uninhabited island—the sole survivor of a shipwreck. Every day he prayed feverishly for God to rescue him. And every day he scanned the horizon for help. No one came. Eventually he managed to build a little hut out of driftwood where he could store his few possessions and get some protection from the sun. At least now he had someplace to call home.

One day, after scavenging for food, he arrived back to find his little hut in flames, smoke rolling up to the sky. Stunned with disbelief and anger, he lifted his face to the sky and cried, "God! How could you do this to me?"

After a fitful night's sleep on the sand, he was awakened by the sound of a ship that had come to rescue him.

"How did you know I was here?" the weary man asked his rescuers.

"We saw your smoke signal," they replied.

Are you distraught with the way things are going in your life? Shipwrecked, with your hut burning to the ground, everything you treasure may seem to be gone. But, friend, remember you still have God. And He knows right where you are. Don't lose heart. Your burning hut may be used by Him to signal help from a source you never thought would come to your rescue.

Many times the writer of the psalms despaired of human help. Yet he knew he could count on God. He wrote, "My flesh and my heart may fail, but God is the strength of my heart and my portion forever" (Psalm 73:26).

Hang on until help comes.

An Experiment

Just six little words—that's all. They're from the Bible, and they're powerful: "Do everything without complaining or arguing" (Philippians 2:14). Six ordinary words simple to understand, but oh so hard to put into action. I challenge you to try to put them into practice today:

#1: Don't complain about anything

#2: Don't argue about anything

How far do you think you'll get into your day before you flunk the challenge? Can you finish breakfast without complaining or arguing? For some of us, complaining starts much earlier than that. Just hearing the alarm clock go off in the morning sparks an objection about having to get up.

Now I wouldn't mind the apostle Paul giving us this instruction...if he just hadn't included the word "everything." Doing *everything* without protest or dispute is really hard. Some situations just seem to call for complaining or arguing. I want to reserve the right to complain under certain conditions.

Just think, though, what could happen in our relationships if we took this verse seriously. How peaceful our marriages and our families would be if we didn't argue. Tonight sit down with your family and show them Philippians 2:14. See if you can get everyone to agree to put it into action for one week. You may even want to make a rule that if anyone complains or argues, he or she has to put a small amount of money in a fund to buy ice cream for the family at the end of the week.

You may be surprised at the difference your experiment will make.

Disappointment—or
God's Appointment?

Back in the early 1800s, Barnabas Shaw made plans to go to Ceylon as a missionary. But instead, the mission organization sent him to Cape Town, South Africa. There he met further disappointment when the governor banned him from preaching. Shaw and his wife deeply wanted to serve the Lord, but two major frustrations in a matter of months had discouraged them.

Not knowing what else to do, the Shaws purchased oxen and a cart, loaded up their possessions and headed for the interior of South Africa. After 27 days, they were met by a group of Hottentots who were on their way to Cape Town to look for the missionary they believed was being sent to teach them the Word of God. Amazingly, their paths had crossed in the dense jungle. The Hottentots then led them 200 miles further inland. The Shaws established a teaching center and eventually spread the gospel to the surrounding areas. The Shaws' disappointments were actually God's appointments for what He wanted to accomplish.[14]

When the apostle Paul planned to go to Asia and Bithynia, his travel itinerary was also thwarted. Instead, he made his way to Troas, where he had a vision of a Macedonian man begging for help. Acts 16:10 says, "We got ready at once to leave for Macedonia, concluding that God had called us to preach the gospel to them." When they arrived in the capital city of Philippi, Paul established a strong church. He later wrote a beautiful letter to this group, which is now called the book of Philippians in our Bible.

Are you dealing with disappointments in your life? Just wait. The last chapter isn't written yet. Your disappointment may be God's appointment to accomplish something outstanding.

Created for a Purpose

While I am convinced that every one of us is here on earth for a reason, whenever I speak on this subject, inevitably the question comes up, "But what about people with disabilities—especially severe disabilities? Does God have a purpose for them? Or did He make a mistake when He made them?"

Let me tell you about John and Christine Haggai's son, Johnny, who was born with severe cerebral palsy. He could not talk or walk or feed himself and required 24-hour-a-day care. He lived for only 24 years.

An intoxicated doctor's negligence caused Johnny to be born with these acute limitations. But his parents chose to accept his birth into their family as God's divine design for them. They devoted countless hours to his care. Both say he was an incredible blessing. Rather than being a burden, he enhanced their lives and inspired them to push on in Christian ministry.

"Chris and I are thoroughly convinced," says Dr. Haggai, "that Johnny came to us in the sovereign and loving will of God. Johnny lived a significant life. Significant not just because there is worth in every person, as there surely is, but…[Johnny] had a role to fill, a destiny to realize."[15]

Our culture strongly values perfection—a beautiful woman, an athletic man, a skillful artist or popular musician. Yet clearly the Bible points to a purpose for each of us being here—whether whole or broken. As an encouragement, Psalm 138:8 says, "The LORD will fulfill [his purpose] for me" (brackets in original). Let Him use you—whatever your limitations—to bless someone today.

A Priceless Gift

E very Sunday night Pastor Eric Denton takes a "Jackets for Jesus" team more than 50 miles from Riverside, California, to the streets of Los Angeles to feed the street people a hot meal and share the love of Jesus with them— people for whom this may be the only gift of love they ever receive. Oh, and yes, if they're cold, they get a good, previously owned jacket as well. Donations come from individuals and organizations who want to help.

I so admire Pastor Eric for doing this after a busy Sunday at his church. Sometimes he surely would rather go home, put his feet up, and rest.

Not too long ago Pastor Eric invited everyone in the food line to bring a well-deserved birthday card the next Sunday for Jodi, the woman who for more than a decade has been in charge of preparing the meals they serve each week. One woman stopped and, placing her hand on Jodi's shoulder, told her she wouldn't be able to be with her for her birthday. The woman then pulled out three filthy, crumpled one dollar bills and pushed them into Jodi's protesting hands.

It was the only money the homeless woman had and was truly a gift from her heart.

Looking at the grimy bills, Pastor Eric thought, *I wonder how many people ever received the gift of a person's entire fortune given in thanksgiving?*

The Bible cautions that "the love of money is a root of all kinds of evil" (1 Timothy 6:10). But Pastor Eric says, "God can make all things good. Last week he turned three dollars into a priceless birthday gift, never to be forgotten."[16]

We each have the opportunity to give. Let's do it out of hearts filled with thankfulness!

A Beautiful Woman

Evelyn Harris was a privileged, beautiful woman—so beautiful, in fact, that men competed for the privilege of painting her portrait. But with her husband, Jesse Brand, she left the luxuries of London to become a missionary among the primitive hill people of India. There a son was born—Paul, who at age nine went away to England for schooling. During this time, his father died from fever, and his mother returned to London a broken woman, beaten down by pain and grief. When he first saw her in London, Paul remembers thinking, *Can this bent, haggard woman possibly be my mother?*

Against all advice, Evelyn insisted on returning to India and pouring out her life nursing the sick, rearing orphans, pulling teeth, clearing jungle land, and preaching the gospel. She traveled constantly, sleeping in a tiny mosquito net shelter. By this time Paul had become a gifted doctor, helping the lepers of India. When his mother broke her hip at age 75, Paul asked, "Shouldn't you think about retiring?" But no argument could dissuade her to slow down.

"Paul, if I leave, who will help the village people? In any

case, why preserve this old body if it's not going to be used where God needs me?" That was her final answer.

Paul later wrote, "In old age Mother was thin and crippled, her face furrowed with deep wrinkles. And yet I can truly say that Evelyn Harris Brand was a beautiful woman to the very end." At age 95 Evelyn died and was buried among her people.[17] As the Bible says, "How beautiful on the mountains are the feet of those who bring good news, who proclaim peace, who bring good tidings, who proclaim salvation" (Isaiah 52:7).

The Prison Walls
of Loneliness

Can you imagine being a prisoner in the infamous Paris Bastille for 15 years? That was the experience of Madame Jeanne Guyon, a member of French nobility. Many others shared that horrible experience during the historic era of infamy in the seventeenth century. But Madame Guyon's attitude made a huge difference. She firmly believed that being in the prison was the will of God. The reality that God was with her helped her survive the terrible living conditions and conquer the loneliness. She had such great delight in God that her spirit soared far above the prison walls. In fact, she said the stones in her prison shone like rubies. Here's what she wrote:

A little bird am I.
Shut out from fields of air,
Yet in my cage I sit and sing
To him who placed me there!
Well pleased a prisoner to be,
Because, my God, it pleaseth Thee.[18]

Madame Guyon chose to accept everything that happened to her as coming from the hand of God. She learned not to fight difficulties but to realize that if God allowed them, He would supply the strength she needed. She also learned that she could have moment-by-moment communication with the Lord that banishes loneliness. He was right there with her.

Are you feeling isolated and alone? Jesus said, "Here I am! I stand at the door and knock. If anyone hears my voice and opens the door, I will come in and eat with him, and he with me" (Revelation 3:20). When you make Him your dearest friend, you too can soar above any prison walls you face.

When Jealousy Isn't Sin

We usually think of jealousy as being a bad thing—a sin. You may be surprised to know that the Bible says God gets jealous. But He's jealous for all the right reasons. You see, God loves deeply, and when you love someone intensely, you are jealous of anything or anyone who would steal away that love.

God warned Moses, "Do not worship any other god, for the LORD, whose name is Jealous, is a jealous God" (Exodus 34:14). If I love anything—any person, any activity, any idea—more than I love God, He sees this as infidelity or unfaithfulness. God says, "I have been grieved by their adulterous hearts" (Ezekiel 6:9)—hearts that prefer something or someone else to Him.

G. Campbell Morgan says jealousy is a word that is very similar to the word "zealous."[19] Another synonym is "passionate," the very opposite of being apathetic or indifferent. God is crazy about us, so He's jealous of our love for Him.

Jealousy can be a good thing. I'm glad to know my husband is jealous of my love—that is, he doesn't want to share my love with anyone else. And that's exactly how God is. His heart is pleased when our love for Him is fervent, real, and passionate! It's hard to admit that sometimes we prefer someone or something else to God. Sometimes it seems our love for God evaporates when the heat is on or the events of the day take precedence. Maybe if we consider that infidelity, we'll think twice before choosing something other than God.

How Big?

Not long ago scientists discovered in space the largest ball of hot gas that had yet been found. "The size and velocity are truly fantastic," said one of the physicists who located it. To cross this big ball of gas, traveling at the speed of light, would take you—hold your breath—3 million years! If you want to look at it another way, it's five billion (5,000,000,000) times larger than our solar system.[20] Astounding!

I get excited when I read about the enormity of creation because I get a hint of how big God is. God is greater by far than this newly discovered object in space. In fact, it's only logical that He is greater than anything He has made. David wrote,

> O LORD, our Lord,
> how majestic is your name in all the earth!
>
> You have set your glory
> above the heavens…
>
> When I consider your heavens,
> the work of your fingers,

the moon and the stars,
which you have set in place,

what is man that you are mindful of him,
the son of man that you care for him?

(Psalm 8:1,3-4).

The heavens are the "work of God's fingers"—almost as if one day God decided to do some arts and crafts, so He created the universe. No wonder David essentially cried out, "In comparison with the heavens, what is man that you care about him?" But God does.

I don't know how big the problem is that you're dealing with today, but I can assure you of two things: God is bigger and He cares. Talk to Him about it right now.

Freedom of Forgiveness

Author Ray Pritchard tells an insightful story:

A wise old monk and his young apprentice were walking together along a trail. Their monastery had a rule forbidding all contact with women, but when they came to a river with a fast-flowing current, they saw an old woman weeping near the shoreline because she could not cross the river on her own. The older monk picked up the woman, and, without a word, carried her to the other side.

The old woman went on her way, and the monk and his apprentice proceeded on their journey. For two-and-a-half hours neither said a word, but on the inside, the young monk was seething. When he could stand it no longer, he blurted out, "My Lord, why did you carry that woman across the river? You know that we are not supposed to touch a woman."

The wise old monk looked down at the young man and said, "I put her down hours ago. Why are you still carrying her?"[21]

Are you carrying a burden from your past? Did someone wound you deeply? They were wrong and you were right...and yet you are still carrying the load. Alan Paton said, "When a deep injury is done to us, we never recover until we forgive."[22] If we're holding a grudge or allowing resentment to live within us, we'll pay the price physically, emotionally, and even spiritually. And these problems will continue to plague us until we forgive. The Bible says, "Be kind and compassionate to one another, forgiving each other, just as in Christ God forgave you" (Ephesians 4:32).

If Jesus could hang on the cross and pray, "Father, forgive them" after all the people did to Him, can we refuse to forgive?

In the Nick of Time

She was at a point of desperation. Deciding that life wasn't worth living any longer, she climbed up to where she could loop a pair of pantyhose over the rafters. Now she was ready to fasten them around her neck and jump. But her radio was on, and suddenly the speaker's words caught her attention. The message was only five minutes long—a program called *Guidelines* that my husband has produced five days a week for more than 40 years. The topic that day was, incredibly, "What God Thinks of Suicide."

Instead of jumping, the woman reached for her phone and called the radio station. The technician airing the program that day answered the call and in the next few moments led her to faith in Christ. Since that time she has visited the station, and it's been confirmed—she is a changed person!

Think of the timing of that incident. The program had been written several months earlier to meet programming deadlines. After the recording session, a Guidelines volunteer listened to be sure there were no grammatical errors or technical blips. Then a CD was produced and mailed to the station. And then there's the fact that the station chose to air that particular program on that particular day. And the program went on the air at exactly the time the woman was taking steps to end her life. That was no accident!

The psalmist wrote, "My times are in your hands" (Psalm 31:15). God makes no mistakes, for He is a God of precision. He can manage the timing in your life. Put your life in His hands and trust Him.

No Greater Love

Robert McQuilken was serving as president of Colum- bia Bible College when his wife, Muriel, developed Alzheimer's disease. Becoming increasingly confused, even- tually she could form only one sentence…but she said it often: "I love you."

After Robert would leave for work, often Muriel would walk to where he was—a one mile round trip that she would sometimes make 10 times a day. At night he would see that her feet were bruised and bloodied. Finally he decided that he could no longer keep his position and care for Muriel, so he resigned the presidency, saying, "Had I not promised, forty-two years before, 'in sickness and in health…till death do us part'?"[23]

McQuilken was criticized. After all, other people could take care of Muriel, but not everyone could fill his shoes at the school. Soon she would not even know who he was, so why should he give up his ministry to care for her?

"It's not that I *have* to," he answered them. "It's that I *get* to. I love her very dearly…It's a great honor to care for such a wonderful person."[24] "As I watch her brave descent into oblivion, Muriel is the joy of my life."[25]

Robert McQuilken's love draws us back to Jesus' love, for that is exactly what He did for us. "Greater love has no one than this, that he lay down his life for his friends" (John 15:13).

We're not always very lovable. In fact, sometimes we're downright difficult. Yet He cares for us—not because He *has* to but because He *wants* to.

God Keeps His Word

Heather Reynolds, founder and director of God's Golden Acre in South Africa, has saved the lives of thousands of children among the Zulu people. In the face of insurmountable odds, she has provided a loving home for hundreds of children with HIV-AIDS and those orphaned by the disease.

At a certain point, God's Golden Acre desperately needed sand to complete the refurbishing of one of the center's buildings. A volunteer, who was an atheist, challenged Heather, "Why don't you ask your God to provide the sand if you have no money to buy some?"

Heather thought, *This young man is quite right. God, why don't You answer our prayers? Do You want me to beg?* She picked up the phone and called the local building supply—for the third time—asking for a load of sand as a donation. She was turned down and adamantly told not to call again.

About half an hour later Heather was disturbed by loud laughter outside on the grounds.

"What's all this about?" asked Heather as she went outside.

"It's your miracle," said the atheist volunteer. "You see that man walking through the gate over there? He's the driver of a 10-ton truck of sand, and he has just broken down at our driveway. He has asked our permission to tip all this sand so his company can tow the truck away." Ironically, it was the same company from which Heather had just asked for sand.[26]

One of Heather's favorite Bible promises is John 14:14: "You may ask me for anything in my name, and I will do it." God keeps His Word!

I Want That!

D o you enjoy watching home-and-garden television programs? I do. I love the creativity of people who design
beautiful landscaping and choose lovely colors and decor for
their homes. One program especially caught my attention.
It's called *I Want That!* The program features new inventions
for the home—all the latest gizmos and appliances. I had
to laugh when I first heard the name of the show because
I recognized that the producers had latched on to a very
human trait. We all tend to want the latest and the best of
everything, whether we need it or not. This human characteristic reminds me of something Richard Foster wrote
in his classic book *Freedom of Simplicity:*

> When taken as a whole, the media commercials con-
> stitute a world view, a rival religious philosophy about
> what constitutes blessedness. We are told by television
> that the most idiotic things will make us insanely
> happy. The purpose of all this media bombardment
> is to increase desire. The plan is to change "That's
> extravagant" into "That would be nice to have," and

then into "I really need that," and finally into "I've got to have it!"[27]

Yes, like Eve, who saw the beautiful fruit on the tree, I find it easy to say, "I want that!" But the apostle Paul reminds us, "Be content with what you have, because God has said, 'Never will I leave you; never will I forsake you'" (Hebrews 13:5).

It's true! When we know we have God and that He will never leave us, we have the most important possession in the world—and really, the only one that matters.

Something Beautiful

An artist began work on what he meant to be the masterpiece of his life. In his mind he knew exactly what he wanted to paint. He was working on the canvas, putting on the drab grays that were to make up the background when a friend came by to see him.

"I plan for this to be the greatest work I've ever done," the artist commented to his friend.

His friend could hardly suppress his laughter. "It looks like one big daub of gray paint," the friend responded.

"Ah," replied the artist, "you cannot see what is *going* to be there. I can."[28]

God knows what He wants to paint on the canvas of your life. As you look at yourself, you may not see much more than a drab daub of paint. But the Divine Artist has an image in mind.

It's not up to the canvas to become a valuable piece of art—it's up to the artist. The canvas itself isn't worth much. But when the artist transfers his vision to the canvas, the work becomes beautiful and valuable.

We can do no better in life than to offer ourselves to

God to create in us what He has in mind. His plans are far greater than ours, for He says, "As the heavens are higher than the earth, so are my ways higher than your ways and my thoughts than your thoughts" (Isaiah 55:9).

Give yourself to the Lord, and He will truly make something beautiful of your life. "He who began a good work in you will carry it on to completion until the day of Christ Jesus" (Philippians 1:6).

The Word of a Gentleman

In 1865, missionary-explorer David Livingstone had to pass through land controlled by a chief who had aggressively been opposing the missionary's work. Livingstone was warned that warriors were in the jungle and creeping toward his camp.

Going alone to his tent, Livingstone opened his Bible to Matthew 28:18-20, a promise on which he had often staked his life. Then he wrote in his journal:

> January 14, 1856. Felt much turmoil of spirit in view of having all my plans for the welfare of this great region and teeming population knocked on the head by savages tomorrow. But I read that Jesus came and said, "All Power is given unto Me in Heaven and in Earth. Go ye therefore, and teach all nations...and lo, I am with you always, even unto the end of the world."
>
> It's the word of a Gentleman of the most sacred and strictest honour, and there's an end on it! I will not cross furtively by night...Nay, verily, I shall take observations for latitude and longitude tonight, though they may be the last. I feel quite calm now, thank God! [29]

The next morning while the chief and his men watched from the jungle's edge, Livingstone instructed the expedition to cross the river. He deliberately chose to be in the last seat in the last canoe, making himself vulnerable to attack. "Tell [the chief] to observe that I am not afraid," said Livingstone. He never looked back. The entire group crossed safely. God kept His Word.

In the chaos of your circumstances, you too can hold on to God's promise to be with you always. You have the word of a Gentleman.

The Disciple Whom Jesus Loved

Five times in the New Testament John is called "the disciple whom Jesus loved." Five times ought to be enough to convince anyone Jesus really loved this man, right? What is interesting, though, is that all five occur in one of the books *John* wrote—the Gospel of John. John uses this expression of himself.

Did Jesus love him? Certainly He did. He loved all of His disciples. Do you think He loved John more than the other disciples? There is no indication of that in the Bible. So was it wrong for John to call himself the disciple whom Jesus loved? I don't think so. The only thing in which he boasted was the fact that Jesus loved him.

Jesus loved John—and He also loves you. Doesn't that make you a "disciple whom Jesus loves"? Have you ever thought of yourself that way? Try saying it to yourself out loud: "I am the disciple whom Jesus loves."

"This is love: not that we loved God, but that he loved us and sent his Son as an atoning sacrifice for our sins" (1 John

4:10). Oh how much God loves us! Karl Barth, a Swiss theologian, was asked about the most profound thing he had learned in his theological studies. He replied, "Jesus loves me, this I know, for the Bible tells me so."

The next time you stand in front of a mirror, look right into your eyes and say, "I am the disciple whom Jesus loves." And then thank Him for that reality.[30]

Welcoming Interruptions

Have you noticed that Jesus never seemed to mind being interrupted? He could accept delays in life because He saw time from an eternal perspective. Jesus knew the past, the present, and the future—all at the same time.

We can't know all that, so we get frustrated when things don't go as planned. We have our day all figured out to accomplish certain things we feel are important. And then along comes an interruption. Nothing is left to do but to trust that somehow God will work His purposes in spite of the hole in our planned activities for the day.

James O. Fraser, who was a missionary in China in the early 1900s, experienced this problem when he needed uninterrupted time for language study. He said,

> I am finding out that it is a mistake to plan to get through a certain amount of work in a certain time. It ends in disappointment, besides not being the right way to go about it...It makes one impatient of interruptions and delay. Just as you are nearly finishing—somebody comes along to sit with you and have a

chat! I think it is well to cultivate an attitude of mind which will enable one to welcome him from the heart and at any time.[31]

Why am I writing about interruptions today? Because I just had a four-hour delay pop up in the middle of my day that totally changed my plans. I'm glad for the scripture that assures me that interruptions are okay: "Many are the plans in a man's heart, but it is the LORD's purpose that prevails" (Proverbs 19:21). If God sends the interruption, then it's a Divine appointment!

I Need Shades

Strolling through the mall, I caught sight of a T-shirt with the catchy slogan, "The future is so bright, I need shades." I couldn't help smiling. In fact, as I continued walking, my whole attitude lightened. Jesus is my Savior, and heaven is my home. No matter how gloomy the present, the future is bright—very bright. One day, when all the problems of this life are over, I'll spend forever and ever with the Lord. What could be more hopeful?

I'm sure that if we could get even a glimpse into heaven, our human eyes would need heavy-duty sunglasses because of the light. The last book of the Bible tells us, "There will be no more night. They will not need the light of a lamp or the light of the sun, for the Lord God will give them light" (Revelation 22:5).

But instead of focusing on the bright future, I tend to focus on the depressing problem I'm dealing with at the moment. I need to put on the sunglasses of faith and look forward with expectancy.

Jesus mastered that principle. The Bible tells us "for the joy set before him," Jesus endured death by crucifixion

(Hebrews 12:2). He bore the darkness of Calvary and its excruciating pain because He knew the light that awaited Him in His Father's presence. We can keep going the same way—enduring pain because of the joy ahead.

If life is bleak around you, turn to Jesus, the Light of the world. Then look ahead, for the future is as bright as the promises of God. You may even want to get yourself one of those T-shirts.

Two Important Words

Kay Warren, wife of pastor and author Rick Warren, says, "In parenting, if you don't insist on anything else, insist that your kids learn to obey two words, 'Come' and 'No.'" She explains that if your children learn to come to you when you call and to accept your no when you have to deny them something they want, they will learn to obey God when He uses those two words.

God calls us, saying, "Come to me, all you who are weary and burdened, and I will give you rest" (Matthew 11:28). But even though we're bone-tired from carrying a heavy load, we tell ourselves that we have no time to come to the Lord. We're much too busy. So we stubbornly muddle through in our own strength. God says "Come," and we say "No."

Other times it's God who says no to us: "Don't do that. It's not good for you." But we interpret that to mean "God doesn't want me to have what I want." Or we chalk it up to "unanswered prayer," thinking God didn't hear or doesn't care. Jesus said, "If you, then, though you are evil, know how to give good gifts to your children, how much more will your Father in heaven give good gifts to those who ask him!" (Matthew 7:11). If we want the best for our own children, surely we can understand that God wants the best for us.

Teach your kids to obey those two key words: "Come" and "No." It's also a great idea to learn to obey those same words yourself when you hear them from your heavenly Father.

Precious

When I was growing up, a friend of ours had a dog she named "Precious." My dad would almost get ill when he heard her call the dog by that name. She was a rather homely little animal—and besides, he reasoned, "Precious" is much too sentimental, gushy, and syrupy for any dog.

Believe it or not, that prompted me to look up the word "precious" in my Bible concordance program to see how the word is used in Scripture. Not surprisingly, it is used of jewels and rare metals, but also in many other ways as well.

When Jacob and Leah's sixth son was born, Leah said, "God has presented me with a precious gift" (Genesis 30:20). Job says that a smile in the time of trouble is precious (Job 29:24), and he should know. Life is called "precious" (Psalm 22:20; 35:17), as is death: "Precious in the sight of the Lord is the death of his saints" (Psalm 116:15). Wisdom is said to be more precious than rubies (Proverbs 3:15; 8:11). God's Word is "more precious than gold" (Psalm 19:10), and so are His "very great and precious promises" (2 Peter 1:4).

It's not surprising that the blood of Christ is called precious (1 Peter 1:19). And Jesus is called the "precious cornerstone" of the church or body of Christ (1 Peter 2:6-7). And, last, Peter speaks of faith as being precious (2 Peter 1:1).

There's one more thing in Scripture that God says is precious: You! God says, "You are precious and honored in my sight...[and] I love you" (Isaiah 43:4). Take that thought with you today!

Stuck in Pain

Is your life right now a "bed of roses"—free of problems?

"Ha! Are you kidding?" That's how many people would respond. "Right now I can't even remember what a rose *smells* like!"

I've noticed through my own painful experiences that sometimes people get *stuck* in their pain. By that I mean we take this attitude: "I refuse to feel better until this situation that can't be changed *is* changed." When we do this, we are painting ourselves into an emotional corner.

When I am stuck in pain, no one is responsible for my feelings except me. I may not be able to change the circumstances, but *I can choose* my attitude toward them. Someone sent me a humorous email called "Attitude Is Everything!"

It seems a woman woke up one morning and noticed she had only three hairs on her head.

"Well," she said, "I think I'll braid my hair today." She did and she had a wonderful day.

The next day she woke up and saw that she had only

two hairs on her head. "Hmm, I think I'll part my hair down the middle today." And she had a grand day.

The next day she woke up and noticed she had only one hair on her head. "Today I'm going to wear my hair in a pony tail." And she had a great day.

The fourth day she woke up and saw that there wasn't a single hair on her head. "Wonderful!" she exclaimed. "I don't have to fix my hair today!"

The Bible says, "Be made new in the attitude of your minds" (Ephesians 4:23). That's good advice for all of us.

Mature Choices

When my pastor husband speaks on "Ten Commandments for Parents of Teens," he says that what teens want and what you want for them is not the same thing. What teens want more than anything else is independence—the right to make their own decisions. On the other hand, what you want for your teens is maturity—the ability to make the *right* decisions.

God says of His people, "If only they were wise and would understand…and discern what their end will be!" (Deuteronomy 32:29). That verse is a great description of maturity—the ability to discern what will be the end results of our decisions. If a person can weigh a situation, looking down the road to see what will be the future result of each possible choice, and then choose the best, he or she has true wisdom and understanding.

Robert Frost's poem "The Road Not Taken" pictures the author coming to a point in life where the road divides into two and he is confronted with a choice:

Two roads diverged in a wood, and I—

I took the one less traveled by,
And that has made all the difference.

No doubt we parents talk too much and don't listen enough. If you are counseling teens who have decisions to make that will affect their futures, spend plenty of time listening to them sort through their questions and thoughts. Ask pertinent questions. Resist the urge to tell them what to do. Get them to think about what the end results will be for each of their choices. And then pray for them. You may be surprised at the mature choices they'll make.

The Committee in Your Head

Jan Johnson says for a long period of time she was plagued by what she calls "the committee that lives in my head." She said there were four people who sat on the committee and continually harassed her.

The first, "Looking Good Kid," always worked hard to be admired. He urged Jan, "Don't make any mistakes, and then I'll be proud of you."

The second committee member that hassled her was "Rescuer." This person continually thought up ways for her to help others so they would have to love her. This resulted in Jan having an impossible-to-keep-up-with schedule.

Committee member number three was "Attitude Police Officer." She was always evaluating Jan, who could never live up to her expectations.

The final member of the committee was "The Grouch," who told her other people should be paying more attention to her. "You poor thing!" he'd protest.[32]

You may have some of these people on the committee

in your head who are utterly impossible to please as they condemn you. How different is this committee from God! Jan found relief when she confronted the committee with the truth that God is not interested in performance but rather in relationships with us.

When thoughts of inadequacy disturb your peace of mind, replace them with biblical truth. "As for God, his way is perfect; the word of the LORD is flawless. He is a shield for all who take refuge in him" (2 Samuel 22:31). You aren't perfect but you have a perfect Savior who can disband the committee in your head.

Keep Rowing

In his painting "The Helping Hand," French artist Emile Renouf shows an old fisherman seated in his rowboat with a little girl next to him. Both the old man and small child have their hands on the large oar as they make their way across the water. From the look on the little girl's face, you can see that she is intense in her effort to help the man row the boat although his strong arms are really doing the work. How like us in our efforts to accomplish what God has given us to do! We sometimes act as if everything depends on us, when really we're merely putting our hands on the oar.

Whatever you're accomplishing, remember to give God credit. He warns that after people become successful, they may be tempted to say, "'My power and the strength of my hands have produced this wealth for me.' But remember the LORD your God, for it is he who gives you the ability to produce wealth" (Deuteronomy 8:17-18).

Maybe right now you're in the middle of a big task. Your hands are on the oar—and you may even be getting blisters. Remember, God's strong hands are also there, and it's His help you need if you're going to finish the job to

His glory. David said many years ago: "The LORD is my strength and my shield; my heart trusts in him, and I am helped" (Psalm 28:7).

"Be strong in the Lord and in his mighty power" (Ephesians 6:10). Keep on rowing—knowing that it's a privilege to work with God.

A Saint?

It happened in the mid-1600s during the reign of Oliver Cromwell. The British government was running out of silver for making coins, so Lord Protector Cromwell sent his soldiers to a local cathedral to look for silver. When they returned from their search, they reported that the only silver they could find was in the statues of the saints standing in the church. "Good!" Lord Cromwell replied. "We'll melt down the saints and put them into circulation."[33]

The Bible refers to all believers as "saints." Paul prays that the Ephesians will "have power, together with all the saints, to grasp how wide and long and high and deep is the love of Christ" (Ephesians 3:18). He speaks of "the riches of [God's] glorious inheritance in the saints" (Ephesians 1:18). He urges them to "always keep on praying for all the saints" (Ephesians 6:18). In Colossians he writes that the previously unknown reality that Christ dwells within us has been disclosed to the saints (Colossians 1:26-27). Jude urged believers to "contend for the faith that was once for all entrusted to the saints" (Jude 3).

You may not think of yourself as a saint because your

idea is that of someone "other worldly" and, well, perfect. In biblical terms, however, a saint is anyone whose sins have been forgiven and to whom Christ has credited His righteousness.

If ever we needed "saints melted down and put into circulation," it is today! Believers are needed who will penetrate our culture in every area and demonstrate by their lives and their love the truth of the gospel of Jesus. The world is looking for people who are real...not perfect.

Why Doesn't God Tell Us?

M any of the "whys" of life are totally beyond our comprehension, such as a toddler run over by a car, a jetliner crash because of birds, deadly storms, and violent earthquakes. Animals don't ask why, they just endure. But God gave humans the ability to ask why. The difficulty is that He created us with enough logic to ask the questions, but not enough insight to understand the answers.

I believe that He set life up this way as a test of faith. If we could understand the answers to all our whys, we wouldn't have to trust Him. Someday we'll understand because we'll have the perspective of eternity. In the meantime, trusting God with the whys is the ultimate test of whether or not we believe He is trustworthy.

So what do you do with all your whys? Ruth Bell Graham said we must lay them at the foot of the cross of Jesus because the cross represents the ultimate why: Why would God send His Son to die for us? What is there about us that is at all lovable? Romans 5:8 says, "God demonstrates his own love for us in this: While we were still sinners, Christ died for us." God's love for us evokes confidence that He has our ultimate good at heart.

Mrs. Graham put it so beautifully when she wrote,

I lay my "whys?"
before Your cross
in worship kneeling,
my mind beyond all hope,
my heart beyond all feeling;
and worshipping,
realize that I
in knowing You,
don't need a "why?"[34]

Finding Comfort

"Tribulation" is a word you probably don't use every day of the week. But you *experience* it nearly every day. "Tribulation" means trouble, problems, hardship, misery, difficulty, distress, ordeals, pain, and suffering. Knowing that, are you now thinking, *I'm an expert in tribulation!* If so, you'll be interested in the background of the word.

When Rome ruled the world, grain was a precious commodity, and threshing grain was part of everyday life. Across the sheaves of cut grain, the Romans pulled a crude cart that was equipped with rollers instead of wheels. Sharp stones and rough bits of iron were attached to these rollers to help separate the husks from the grain. This cart was called a tribulum—from which we get our word "tribulation"— a fitting picture of how troubles grind on us and put us under pressure.

A Roman farmer, however, didn't use his tribulum to destroy the grain—only to refine it. So too God uses our troubles to make us stronger. God's Word says that "tribulation brings about perseverance" (Romans 5:3 NASB).

The apostle Paul wrote that God "comforts us in all our

troubles" (2 Corinthians 1:4), that is, He strengthens us and sustains us. This relates directly to one of the names given to the Holy Spirit: "Comforter." Bible teacher G. Campbell Morgan says that comfort means more than reassurance or consolation. It means reinforcing the person and sustaining him. It means coming to his side to help. God's comfort is no less than His strengthening companionship and upholding power.[35]

If you're experiencing tribulation, ask for God's help. You'll find that the Comforter will strengthen and encourage you.

The One Who
Lifts You Up

Karl Crowe tells of a missionary who noticed that in the Bible of the tribe she was working with, the word "idinide" had been used for the English word "Savior."[36] "Idinide" meant "picker upper." The missionary thought, *This is not the right word!*

Then one day a tribal woman gave birth to a child, and the missionary was asked to visit and be the idinide or "picker upper." She found the newborn baby on the jungle floor and the mother lying in a hammock above.

"What am I supposed to do?" she asked the mother.

"You pick up and wash the baby," the mother replied.

Getting water from a nearby stream, the missionary cleaned him as best she could. "Now what?" she asked.

"Take the baby to the village and present him to his father," the mother responded.

The missionary found the father and informed him that he had a newborn son. Suddenly she began to understand why idinide had been used for Savior. No finer word picture could be used to show what Jesus does when He finds us wherever we are—sometimes in the gutter, sometimes in our loneliness, but always in our sin. He cleans us up, cuts the cord that bound us to our sinful lives, and finally brings us to the Father, saying, "This is Your new adopted child. I gave My life to bring her into Our family!"

God "raises the poor from the dust and lifts the needy from the ash heap" (Psalm 113:7). "The LORD upholds all those who fall and lifts up all who are bowed down" (Psalm 145:14). Jesus...Idinide...Savior...praise His holy name.

A Memory Reminder

When Joshua was ready to lead the Israelites across the Jordan River to enter the land the Lord had promised them so many years before, God said to him, "Choose twelve men from among the people, one from each tribe, and tell them to take up twelve stones from the middle of the Jordan…and to carry them over with you and put them down at the place where you stay tonight" (Joshua 4:2-3).

So Joshua called together 12 men and did as God commanded. When they camped at Gilgal, Joshua set up the 12 stones. He told the people,

> In the future when your descendants ask their fathers, "What do these stones mean?" tell them…the LORD your God did to the Jordan just what he had done to the Red Sea when he dried it up before us until we had crossed over. He did this so that all the peoples of the earth might know that the hand of the LORD is powerful and so that you might always fear the LORD your God" (verses 21,23-24).

These stones were a memorial to God's loving care.

Do you have an item that is a reminder of something special God did for you in the past? I once heard about a family who had survived a severe auto accident and were so thankful they were all still alive that they took pieces of the car wreckage and formed them into a collage on their wall so that in the future when people asked about it, they could tell of God's miraculous protection. I think that's a great idea!

Whether it's a gift someone gave you, or a picture, or a plaque, it can be a reminder of God's provision—a reminder to you and a conversation starter for you to tell someone else your story. Maybe one day your grandchildren will ask, "What does this mean, Grandma?" And you'll be able to tell them how God answered your prayers.

57 Cents

Hattie May Wiatt, who lived in the 1800s, wanted to go to Sunday school, but there was no room in the classroom.[37] The pastor saw her crying and asked what was wrong. He took her into the Sunday School room and said, "Hattie, we're going to have a larger Sunday school when we get the money—large enough for all the children."

Sadly, Hattie May became sick and died. After the funeral, her mother handed the pastor a small bag containing 57 cents that Hattie had gathered toward another building for the children. At church the pastor stated they had the first gift toward the new Sunday school building—Hattie May's 57 cents. As a testament to Hattie's determination, the pastor converted her 57 cents into pennies and auctioned them to raise money for the new Sunday school room. When 54 of those cents were returned to him by the people who bought them (along with their contributions), the pastor had them framed and placed where they could be seen. A society was formed, dedicated to making Hattie May's 57 cents grow, and soon a nearby house was purchased with the money given in honor of her gift.

But there's more! The church was too small, so the pastor followed Hattie's example. He went to the owner of a nearby lot and told him they had only 54 cents in their building fund, but they would like to buy that lot. Incredibly the owner took the pennies as a down payment.

And one last thing. The Sunday school building bought as the result of Hattie May's 57 cents later held the first classes of Temple University, which now enrolls more than 27,000 students.[38]

Like the little boy who gave his lunch to Jesus (John 6:5-13), Hattie May's gift was multiplied to bless thousands.

What do you have to give?

When God Couldn't Look

For years Dr. Margaret Brand served as a missionary eye surgeon in southern India. In the rural areas she would sometimes do a hundred cataract surgeries in a single day. In one instance where there was no electricity, a 12-year-old boy was given the job of holding a large flashlight so that its beam gave the doctor enough light to do her work. Dr. Brand was dubious that he would be able to stand up to the trauma of seeing eyes sliced open and stitched, but for the first five operations he did his job impressively. During the sixth, however, he faltered.

"Little brother, show the light properly," Dr. Brand instructed. But she could see that he simply couldn't bear to look at the eye. When she asked him if he was feeling well, she saw that tears were running down cheeks. "Oh, doctor, I cannot look," replied the lad. "This one, she is my mother."[39]

When Jesus was hanging on the cross, God the Father couldn't look. Jesus cried out, "My God, my God, why have you forsaken me?" (Matthew 27:46). A great shadow had come between Jesus and the Father. Jesus was lonely on that cross because of you and me. God had to turn His eyes away from His Son for those moments because of our sin. You see, "God made him who had no sin to be sin for us, so that in him we might become the righteousness of God" (2 Corinthians 5:21).

Have you thanked Jesus recently for being willing to pay such a great price?

God Hears You

Jesus was tired. He had been teaching large crowds of people who were gathered at the Sea of Galilee. When evening came, He said to His disciples, "Let us go over to the other side [of the lake]." So they left the crowd behind and took Him by boat across the lake. Jesus was so tired that during the journey He put His head on a cushion and went to sleep.

Very quickly a strong squall came up, and the waves broke over the boat, so that it was nearly swamped. Jesus slept on. Finally the disciples woke him. "Teacher, don't you care if we drown?" they asked. Immediately Jesus stood up, rebuked the wind, and said to the waves, "Quiet! Be still!" And the wind died and the water became completely calm (Mark 4:35-39).

To me, the remarkable truth from this story is not merely that the storm obeyed the command of Jesus. That *is*, of course, amazing! But the thought that comforts me is that although the howling of the wind and the splash of the waves didn't waken Jesus, the cries of the people in trouble did.

Like a mother who can tune out the din of traffic on

the street outside but waken at the slightest whimper of her baby, the Lord responded to the needs and fears and cries of His children. And He does the same today. Isn't that comforting? The psalmist said, "The righteous cry out, and the LORD hears them" (Psalm 34:17). The God of heaven hears when you call. If the storm in your life is about to swamp your boat, cry out to the One who said to the wind and waves, "Quiet! Be still"…and they obeyed.

Name a Star

Do you want to give someone a unique gift? Starting at $25 you can name a star in your friend's honor. If you enter "name a star" in your Internet browser, you'll find a number of sites that offer to do just that. Now, before you get too excited, let me say that only the International Astronomical Union has the right to officially name celestial objects, and they don't give names—they use a numbering system. Even one of the star-naming websites admits, "Naming a star is a symbolic gesture."[40]

A recent study by Australian astronomers says that there are 70 sextillion stars—that's a 7 followed by 22 zeros, or 70,000 million million million.[41] Mind-boggling, isn't it? How did they arrive at this number? Using two of the most powerful telescopes in the world, scientists surveyed a strip of sky. Within this strip, some 10,000 galaxies were pinpointed and detailed measurements of their brightness taken to calculate how many stars they contained. That number was then multiplied by the number of similarly sized strips needed to cover the entire sky, and then multiplied again out to the edge of the visible universe.

Only God knows exactly how many stars there are. The Bible says, "He determines the number of the stars and calls them each by name" (Psalm 147:4).

If God can keep track of the names of 70 sextillion stars, don't you think He can keep track of the details of your life? Thank Him today that He is bigger than any problem you face. Then go about your work, trusting Him to guide you just as He guides the 70 sextillion stars in the sky.

Use Your Talent

George Washington Carver was an American botanist back in the 1900s. He became famous for discovering 300 uses for the lowly peanut. As one story tells it, Carver once asked the Lord about the universe:

"Lord, what is the universe?" The Lord said, "George, that's too big for your little head. Suppose you let me take care of the universe." Greatly humbled, the scientist asked, "Then, Lord, if the universe is too big for me to understand, please tell me, what is a peanut?" And then the Lord answered, "Now, George, you've got something your own size. A peanut can understand a peanut; go to work on the peanut while I run the universe."[42]

Carver discovered that growing peanuts put indispensable nitrogen back into nutrient-depleted soil. He went on to find practical uses for the crop. Carver made cheese, milk, butter, flour, ink, dyes, soap, stains, and many other substances from peanuts.

Yes, running the universe is far too big for us to handle.

But we can go to work on the opportunities the Lord has put in our paths. He doesn't ask us to do what we can't do. The talents, abilities, and aptitudes God has given us are like trust funds dedicated to honoring Him. "Now it is required that those who have been given a trust must prove faithful" (1 Corinthians 4:2).

Maybe He has given you motivational skills. Or artistic talents. Or computer abilities. Maybe the trust God has given you is the family you're raising or the work you're doing. Whatever it is, know that you *can* fulfill the purposes for which God created you because He will help you. So go for it!

Procrastinating

The slogan on the T-shirt said, "Procrastinators, Unite—Tomorrow." Can you relate to that? Most of us are very good at putting off until tomorrow what we don't want to do today. Some of us even go so far as to make lists of what we know we should do. We carefully arrange the tasks in order of importance—and then totally ignore the list and do what we wanted to do in the first place. I know because I'm a procrastinator.

Dr. John Perry, a professor in Stanford University's philosophy department, says,

> The key idea is that procrastinating does not mean doing absolutely nothing. Procrastinators seldom do absolutely nothing; they do marginally useful things, like…sharpening pencils or making a diagram of how they will reorganize their files when they get around to it. Why does the procrastinator do these things? Because they are a way of not doing something more important.[43]

For years I've admired the way my husband does the most

important tasks first. In fact, if there is something he doesn't want to do, he does that first to get it out of the way.

Today I found a scripture that really spoke to my heart: "I will hasten and not delay to obey your commands" (Psalm 119:60). There's no wiggle room in that verse! Hasten and not delay! Well, if God wants me to do it, I'd better get at it. That is very good advice for a procrastinator like me. How about for you?

Temptation

In one form or another, temptation comes to all of us. We've all felt the intense desire to do something we knew we shouldn't. One of the best descriptions I've ever read of temptation was written by Wawa Ponce. She gets very graphic, so be prepared. Ms. Ponce says, "Temptation is a luscious, chocolate-coated morsel that conceals a dozen wriggling maggots inside."[44] (Hey, I warned you!)

Yes, temptation looks good on the outside, and giving in often brings momentary pleasure. Even the Bible mentions "the pleasures of sin" (Hebrews 11:25). But after you've given in, the results are pretty disgusting. Pleasure is usually short lived, and disappointment always follows.

Sometimes we close our eyes to the existence of temptation in our lives, saying, "Well, temptation isn't something that really bothers me. I've never wanted to murder anyone or to cheat big time." But what about the temptation to ignore God? To get revenge? To pretend to be something you're not? To want what someone else has? Does that hit a little closer to home?

The good news is that we don't have to give in to *any*

temptation. "No temptation has seized you except what is common to man. And God is faithful; he will not let you be tempted beyond what you can bear. But when you are tempted, he will also provide a way out so that you can stand up under it" (1 Corinthians 10:13).

God is really the one we're sinning against when we give in to temptation—regardless of its size. When Joseph was tempted by Potiphar's wife to commit adultery, he turned from her and responded, "How...could I do such a wicked thing and sin against God?" (Genesis 39:9). Why not ask yourself that the next time temptation tries to strike?

The Beauty of Encouragement

Yesterday I met a friend I haven't seen in quite a long time. She's a beautiful lady—one of those people who is slender and dresses impeccably. Her natural loveliness captures people's attention. But she has another characteristic that I think is the true secret to her attractiveness. She always makes the person she is talking to feel special. Whenever I meet her, she has a ready word that is complimentary and encouraging. I go away from talking with her feeling that *I* am special too. Author and Bible teacher Anne Ortlund says, "There are two kinds of personalities in this world, and you are one of the two. People can tell which, as soon as you walk into a room: your attitude says either 'Here I am' or 'There you are.'"[45]

Often we're so needy ourselves that we're impatient to tell other people how hard we have it. Knowing that selfish tendency, Pastor Jim George advises, "With every encounter, make it your aim that people are better off for having been in your presence. Try in every encounter to give something to the other person."[46] Good advice, isn't it?

At least three times in the New Testament we're reminded to "encourage one another." So let's get practical. What words of encouragement can you give today to one of your family members? And how about a coworker or even your boss? Or maybe words won't be the only way you encourage someone who needs a lift. A handful of flowers might brighten a person's day. Or a short note saying how special he or she is. Or an email. Or a hug. You can do it—I know you can!

What Are Blessings?

Larry Crabb is a well-known author and psychologist. He shared about the day in the hospital when the doctor told him they had found a mass the size of a tennis ball near his stomach, and that it was likely malignant. From his window that evening he noticed a Starbucks across from the hospital. He imagined a Christian couple there sipping decaf lattes before they drove home, snuggled together, and then got up the next morning for church. He remembers thinking, *They have the abundant life; I have cancer. It's not fair.* That night God spoke to his heart. Larry shared, "I was more aware of my desires for health and good times...That night the cobwebs cleared, and my eyes focused. I realized that I wanted God more than anything or anyone else, with my whole being...*That night I experienced the presence of God.* What more—or less—could I want?"

We think we're closest to God when everything is going well—that smooth sailing in our lives is a sign of God's blessing. Have you defined God's blessings? Are they health, good times, contentment? Have we lost sight of the fact that Larry Crabb rediscovered? That the greatest blessing is knowing God? Larry says, "Every hard thing we endure can put us in touch with our desire for God, and every trial can strengthen that desire until it becomes the consuming passion of our life. Then comes the experience of God...it's the source of our deepest joy, the real point of living."[47]

Jesus said, "Now this is eternal life: that they may know you, the only true God, and Jesus Christ, whom you have sent" (John 17:3). That's truly the greatest blessing of our lives!

A Scary Prayer?

Sometimes when you're reading a book, a single phrase jumps off the page and catches your attention. That's what happened to me this week. I was reading Jill Briscoe's book *The Deep Place Where Nobody Goes*, and the phrase that stood out was in the middle of a conversation that Jill was having with God. The phrase? "Spend me."[48]

I thought, *That's a very courageous request to pray to God—that phrase, "Spend me." Who knows what God will ask a person to do who prays that? Do I really want God to "spend me"?* The idea is intriguing. What would God do with our lives if every day we truly offered every single part of it to Him to use as He wills? What if our only thought during the day was "Lord, take this moment, this energy I have, and use it any way You wish"?

When you think about it, isn't it really a privilege to offer ourselves to God for Him to spend? The Bible says that Christ died for all, "that those who live should no longer live for themselves but for him who died for them and was raised again" (2 Corinthians 5:15).

It may be scary for you to think of praying "Spend me."

"That means I won't have any say over what happens in my life," you might reason. And yes, that's right. God would be in charge. But don't think you'll be wiped out like a sentence a teacher erases off the chalkboard. If God spends your life, you'll achieve the purpose for which you were created. Nothing wasted. Nothing lost. Everything gained.

Yes, Lord, spend me!

When Life Isn't Fair

I was asked to speak to a group of women on how to cope with infidelity, alcoholism, or abuse. I was unqualified to speak from personal experience, so my walking partner, Terri, came up with a plan. She said, "Why don't I set you up to talk to some of my friends who have found God's strength to survive this kind of pain?" I agreed, and Terri did just that. For a week I listened to people's stories and took notes. Drawing on those interviews, I'd like to share five of the principles for women enduring or living these serious problems.

- *Don't blame yourself but accept the responsibility to change the future.* If the situation is dangerous, don't hesitate to get you and your children out of harm's way until the situation is resolved and it's safe.

- *Learn to speak the truth in love* (Ephesians 4:15). Your goal is to learn to be assertive—loving but firm, setting boundaries with consequences for breaking them.

- *Make God your source of esteem.* God's unconditional love will save you from despair.

- *Find the support of other Christian women.* One woman found a prayer partner who would call her every morning and pray with her on the phone.

- *Seek an intimate relationship with God.* A woman living with abuse came to a point where she totally abandoned her life to God. She would withdraw within her own heart to talk to God in prayer. By praying without ceasing she found strength to endure and wisdom to know what to do about the situation.

As you work toward a solution, be assured God will not waste your suffering but use it to make you more like Christ, conforming you "to the likeness of his Son" (Romans 8:29).

In the Dark

I'm always fascinated by people's stories about how God met them at a point of desperation and helped them. Take the Elegados, for instance. In the mining business during the Japanese occupation of the Philippines, Mr. Elegado was the only Filipino to be allowed to drive into "sensitive areas." To pass checkpoints, he had to have a special Japanese sticker on his car.

Eventually, however, he was arrested by the Japanese and taken to prison. For months his wife left their children every weekend to search for her husband. She knew that if she didn't find him he would probably die because the prison rations were so poor. Her heart cried out, *If there is a God—if You are really alive—help me.*

At the end of eight months of searching, she found him. She brought food to him regularly for the next two years of imprisonment he endured in that dark place. And ever since that experience, she and her husband have been dedicated to the Lord.

There is a postscript to the story. The Japanese imprisonment, horrible as it was, saved Mr. Elegado's life. Filipino guerrillas had decided to kill him because of the Japanese sticker on his car—but Mr. Elegado was safe in prison.

When we are in a very dark place, perhaps the darkness is only the shadow of God's hand shielding us from greater danger. Psalm 91 says, "He who dwells in the shelter of the Most High will rest in the shadow of the Almighty...He will cover you with his feathers, and under his wings you will find refuge" (verses 1 and 4).

Aging Gracefully

My son, Steve, says there are three stages to life—youth, middle age, and "My, you're looking well today!" Like it or not, we eventually get to that third stage of life. The problem is that our culture values the new and discards the old. But that isn't God's perspective. He has great promises for our older years. He says, "Even to your old age and gray hairs I am he...who will sustain you. I have made you and I will carry you" (Isaiah 46:4).

How do we age gracefully? By the G-R-A-C-E of God!

Get rid of the garbage. Give up your grudges. Deal with the past and let it go.

Realize your value in God's sight doesn't diminish with age. The Lord says that as believers, we're part of His body: "Those parts of the body that seem to be weaker are indispensable" (1 Corinthians 12:21-22).

Appreciate your life experiences. Share what you've learned with younger people.

Continue to serve. Many look at retirement as a new

life of leisure and self-indulgence. Psalm 92:14 says, "[The righteous] will still bear fruit in old age."

Expect God to honor His Word. Has God been faithful to you so far? Isaiah 41:10 is still true: "So do not fear, for I am with you; do not be dismayed, for I am your God. I will strengthen you and help you; I will uphold you with my righteous right hand."

There you have it: G-R-A-C-E. God's grace, which is indispensable for our aging years.

I Don't Wanna

A young mom who was having a frustrating week wrote me saying, "I'm in a 'kicking, screaming, I don't wanna do it' mood this week." I can certainly identify with her. Sometimes I go so far as to get my week totally organized and then I look at the number one item on my to-do list and think, *I don't want to do this. In fact, I'm not going to do it!*

In the Bible there's a word for this: "disobedience." Oh, I don't like to call it that. But doing God's will in the present moment is all-important because this is really the only moment we have. Joe Stowell says, "Followers [of Christ] can reduce all of life to the question, 'What is it that my Father in Heaven wants for my life in this moment?'"[49] So, doing what I ought to do when I ought to do it really means, "Do I love God enough to put His will above my own—right now?"

It's okay to vent to God and tell Him exactly how you feel. In fact, it's a lot better than taking it out on anybody and everybody around you. If you don't face up to it, you'll stuff the feelings inside—and eventually quit exercising, waste time, watch too much TV, and get even angrier or depressed. But after we tell God how we feel, we still have to admit that the issue is really obedience or disobedience. That's when we must settle it with Him.

Jesus said, "The spirit is willing, but the body is weak" (Mark 14:38). You're so right, Lord. Please help me. My spirit is willing, but oh, this body!

Giving

How much of your money should you give to church and Christian ministries? That's kind of a personal question, isn't it? But the Bible gives clear instructions: "Each man should give what he has decided in his heart to give, not reluctantly or under compulsion, for God loves a cheerful giver" (2 Corinthians 9:7).

Growing up as a preacher's kid, I sometimes sat by myself in church because my dad was leading the service and my mom was playing the organ. One Sunday one of the choir members left her purse in the seat next to mine while she joined the choir. After the choir sang, she would sit with me during the sermon. When offering time came, she watched helplessly from the choir as I opened her purse and took out money to give "for her." I have no memory of how much "she" gave, and I don't know how cheerfully "she" gave.

In the Old Testament giving was to be a tithe—that is, 10 percent of a person's income for the Lord. And when you consider the Old Testament tithe, it really wasn't totally fair. If a person made $500 a month and gave $50 of it, it was a sacrifice. But if a rich person made $50,000 a month and gave $5,000 of it, he still had $45,000 left to spend. But in the New Testament Paul wrote, "On the first day of every week, each one of you should set aside a sum of money *in keeping with his income*" (1 Corinthians 16:2).

Famous Bible teacher G. Campbell Morgan wrote, "Test all your giving by your own prosperity."[50] This is a good rule for deciding how much money to give.

Confessing to the Devil

Okay, you know you've done something God isn't happy about. And let's be honest…it's called "sin." But you also know that Christ died for your sins. So you've confessed this sin to God, and He's forgiven you. "If we confess our sins, he is faithful and just and will forgive us our sins" (1 John 1:9). That clears your conscience, right?

Well, maybe not. When you open your eyes the next morning, you may still have nagging feelings of guilt. You don't *feel* forgiven. So you confess your sin again and ask God to forgive you. You may repeat this vicious cycle over and over.

The devil is the one who makes you feel guilty for forgiven sin because he is a liar. He is called "the accuser of our brothers, who accuses them before our God day and night" (Revelation 12:10). John says, "When [the devil] lies, he speaks his native language, for he is a liar and the father of lies" (John 8:44).

God isn't accusing you or not letting you rest in His forgiveness. When God has forgiven you, it's done…it's over. "There is now no condemnation for those who are in

Christ Jesus" (Romans 8:1). Isn't that great news? And the Bible says we can "demolish arguments and every pretension that sets itself up against the knowledge of God, and we take captive every thought to make it obedient to Christ" (2 Corinthians 10:5). Resist the devil's lies when he accuses you, and accept the truth of God's forgiveness. Joy will replace your false feelings of guilt.

When a Kernel
of Wheat Dies

W hy? Why did Dennis have to die?" The question
screamed in Jean Galang's mind. That 14-year-old boy
had been full of life. But in the church's summer camp, of
all places, Dennis had drowned in the swimming pool. In
a daze of disbelief and heartbreak, the camp was shut down
and everyone went home.

"I could not stop struggling with [God's] method of
bringing about His purposes," Jean recalls. Yet she says, "I
finally accepted and learned to trust God's ways no matter
what and to ultimately let God be God."[51]

As the weeks went by, Jean thought a great deal about
what had happened.

> As camp staff, we took pride in coming up with a great
> camp to teach our young people some valuable lessons
> in life. Instead, God came up with His own plan to
> teach all of us through the life of His precious child,
> Dennis...The incident made an impact on all of our
> lives far greater than a four-day camp would have.

Jesus said, "I tell you the truth, unless a kernel of wheat falls to the ground and dies, it remains only a single seed. But if it dies, it produces many seeds" (John 12:24).

Dennis was, no doubt, that kernel of wheat. Although his life on this earth was short, the effectiveness of his life was multiplied in the lives of students and staff alike. Never will he be forgotten.

Most of us think of the long life as the successful life. But God may have other plans. What matters most is our influence in light of eternity.

Stressed Out

I have come to accept that life moves at such a fast pace that stress can't be totally avoided. Humorists have suggested the following ways of handling stress:

- Fill out your tax forms with Roman numerals.

- Leaf through *National Geographic* magazine and draw underwear on the natives.

- Make lists of things you've already done.

If you are under stress, you may need lists to remind you of almost everything. Scientists have discovered that stress physically affects your body's chromosomes and makes you age. What happens, researchers learned, is that constant stress causes the tiny caps on the cells' chromosomes that govern cell regeneration to get smaller. When the tiny caps get too short, the cell stops dividing and eventually dies.

Researchers found that the greater people perceived their stress to be, the "older" their cells became. And those who didn't perceive their lives as stressful? Stress didn't age them nearly as much, says Dr. Thomas Peris, director of the project.[52]

The study cited real-life examples of people living well into their 80s and 90s who had successfully coped with stress in a number of ways, including sports, games, humor, optimism, a sense of purpose, close friendships, music, finding meaning in life, and prayer.

When I read that list, I couldn't help thinking about what Paul said to the Philippians: "Finally, brothers, whatever is true, whatever is noble, whatever is right, whatever is pure, whatever is lovely, whatever is admirable—if anything is excellent or praiseworthy—think about such things... And the God of peace will be with you" (Philippians 4:8-9). Yes, a close relationship with the Lord is the best stress-buster we have!

Room Enough for God

Mary Southerland tells about visiting Amish country in Pennsylvania one summer. The Amish are a conservative Christian group who dress simply and plainly, do their work and live without the use of electricity, cars, and tractors, and their homes are well-known for simple furnishings. Mary said she enjoyed every minute spent in their carefully ordered world.

Wanting to buy a souvenir to remind them of these peaceful days, she and her husband traveled down some of the country back roads. Finally she spotted a small, white sign that said "Amish Crafts" on the fence of a quaint house. The porch was filled with lovely handmade items. Walking up the stone walk, they were greeted by a woman with a beautiful smile.

The house was sparsely furnished, but the homeowner described her life with words such as "calm, uncomplicated, and serene." When asked why she had chosen such a lifestyle, she responded with words of wisdom: "I have discovered that when my life and my heart get too crowded, there is not enough room for God."

What a thought to ponder! Mary reminds us, "It is so easy to relegate our spirituality to religious activity when all [God] wants is to spend time with us."[53] If our lives are too crowded for God, they're too crowded—period. If you want to change that, start spending time with the Lord. You may be amazed at the peace that comes to your heart. An anonymous poet wrote:

> We mutter and sputter,
> We fume and we spurt;
> We mumble and grumble;
> Our feelings get hurt;
> We can't understand things;
> Our vision grows dim,
> When all that we need
> Is a moment with Him.[54]

Living Sacrifices

It was one of those days when I felt pressured by too much to do, but I was working hard to complete each task. Just then my husband asked me if I had time to run an errand for him. Something flared up inside of me, and in my mind I immediately answered him with a very firm no, even though my answer wasn't audible. I'm sure by the look on my face he detected that I didn't want to do what he needed to have done.

As I quickly thought it over, I realized that I was the logical one to run the errand. After all, I had more available time than he did. So I told him I would do it and started for the car. But inside I was still resentful at being interrupted.

I climbed into the driver's seat, and as I started the car, I switched on the radio. Immediately I heard these words: "Have you ever presented your body to the Lord as a living sacrifice?" *Okay, Lord,* I thought. *I hear You.* In Romans 12:1 Paul says, "Therefore, I urge you, brothers, in view of God's mercy, to offer your bodies as living sacrifices, holy and pleasing to God." Yes, I had made that commitment.

But doing it in a beautiful, candlelit service is one thing. Living out that commitment in everyday life is quite another thing. I confessed my lack of willingness and asked God for His forgiveness.

At one time or another you too may have offered your life to the Lord as a living sacrifice. But maybe you, like me, need to climb back on the altar.

Who's Going to Remember?

Since I get a bit uptight when guests are coming for dinner, my friend sent me this advice:

When you start to have stressful feelings, just say one of the following things:

- "Oh, who cares anyway!" No one ever notices the things that bother you, such as unmatching table napkins or overcooked fish. They're too worried about themselves to notice.

- "Big deal!" If someone comes over and notices that your bedroom is messy and there is toothpaste on the mirror, just tell them that perhaps someone used your room.

- "Just forget it!" This one is appropriate when everything is going smoothly for your summer dinner party—until the doorbell rings and you noticed rain drizzling all over your beautifully set table.

- "In ten years, who's going to remember?" This one is handy when, on the day of an important meeting, you have an allergy attack and break out in hives.

What is really worth getting concerned about anyway? A child with a fever—yes! Your shoes that don't go with your outfit—no! Your husband is losing his job—yes! Jesus said to His hostess in Bethany, "Martha, Martha...you are worried and upset about many things" (Luke 10:41). Whatever the frustrations of life you're dealing with, remember it's people who count with God—and they should with us too.

Sometimes we're like the bride who is so heartbroken that her wedding wasn't "picture perfect" that she forgets she still got the groom! Hug the people you love and forget the imperfections. Who cares anyway? Big deal! In 10 years, who's going to remember?

DARLENE SALA

Gossip

A bit of juicy gossip seems very satisfying. "What dainty morsels rumors are. They are eaten with great relish!" (Proverbs 18:8 TLB). Come on, now. Have you *never* been a bit excited being one of the first to hear some salacious tidbit about a person you didn't like very much?

We can be so self-righteous. My daughter says, "Christians don't gossip; they just share prayer requests." I'm afraid that all too often she's right. When a group of us sit in a circle to pray together, we often spend more time talking about people who need prayer than praying for them.

God hates gossip. The Bible describes godless, sinful people by saying they "have become filled with every kind of wickedness, evil, greed and depravity...envy, murder, strife, deceit and malice. *They are gossips*" (Romans 1:29).

You and I can do something to bring an end to gossip. Proverbs 26:20 says, "Without wood a fire goes out; without gossip a quarrel dies down." So make it a rule in your life to be the stopping point of gossip, rumor, and scandal. If you're tempted to add fuel to the fire by passing on that morsel you've just heard, write Ephesians 4:29 on a sticky note and keep it where you can see it often: "Do not let any unwholesome talk come out of your mouths, but only what is helpful for building others up according to their needs, that it may benefit those who listen."

Let's ask God to help us squelch words that might hurt.

Pleasure That Lasts

When you think of kids opening gifts at Christmas—what a picture of fun! But all too soon the special day is over. And they know it will be another whole year before Christmas comes again. Frances Ridley Havergal wrote, "You never had a pleasure that lasted. You look forward to a great pleasure, and it comes, and then, very soon it is gone, and you can only look back upon it. The very longest and pleasantest day you ever had came to an end."[55]

However, the psalmist says to God, "You will fill me with joy in your presence, with eternal pleasures at your right hand" (Psalm 16:11). Eternal pleasures found in God's presence! Ultimately, lasting pleasure is found only in an intimate, close relationship with God.

A poor Methodist woman of the eighteenth century wrote,

> I do not know when I have had happier times in my soul, than when I have been sitting at work, with nothing before me but a candle and a white cloth, and...with God in my soul...I rejoice in being exactly what

I am—a creature capable of loving God...I get up and look for a while out of the window, and gaze at the moon and stars, the work of an Almighty hand. I think of the grandeur of the universe, and then sit down, and think myself one of the happiest beings in it.[56]

Eternal pleasure comes when you're growing ever closer to the Lord, getting to know Him better each day. That's a privilege—and a pleasure worth pursuing.

The Sin No One Criticizes

What is the sin no one criticizes? Busyness. In fact, we usually think of a busy person as being ambitious and—well, important. We think of busyness as the opposite of laziness. And since none of us wants to be thought of as lazy, we're quite willing to be busier than we probably ought to be.

So how do we set priorities? Most of us grew up thinking that Christian priorities should be:

Jesus first,
Others second,
and then me last.

But I don't believe this is biblical. According to Scripture, our priorities should all be on a horizontal line with God over all. Why not take a piece of paper, turn it sideways, and write "God" at the top. Under that, draw a straight line all the way across the paper. Write down your responsibilities on that line, including family times and recreation. All are important! The way to determine your priorities is to ask

God and listen to Him about what He wants you to be doing at any given point in your day.

If you merely put God first in your life, when you spend time with Him in the morning, you might check Him off as "done" for the day. If you only put God at the center of your life, He may have little impact on the periphery. But if you put Him *over* all of your life, you will be checking with Him continually to see if you're doing what's best for you each moment of your day. Jesus said, "My food...is to do the will of him who sent me and to finish his work" (John 4:34). Let it be your food too. When God speaks to you about priorities, take a definite step in obedience.

Yet I Will Rejoice

The prophet Habakkuk lived in a time of uncertainty. Babylon was growing as a world power, and the people of Judah were afraid they were in for hard times. Yet for all the questions that were raised about the future, the prophet ends his writings with a confident declaration that is a song of encouragement:

> Though the fig tree does not bud
> and there are no grapes on the vines,
>
> though the olive crop fails
> and the fields produce no food,
>
> though there are no sheep in the pen
> and no cattle in the stalls,
>
> yet I will rejoice in the LORD,
> I will be joyful in God my Savior
>
> (Habakkuk 3:17-18).

Do you mind if I paraphrase this for today's time?

Though the gross national product should not rise,
and there be no pay increase this year,

though the yield of the stock market should fail,
and retirement benefits should end,

though G-20 negotiations should be broken off,
and there be no hope of peace in the world,

yet, I will rejoice in the LORD,
I will be joyful in God my Savior.

I have an assignment for you. Before you go to sleep tonight, read Habakkuk 3:17-18 and write your own paraphrase that fits *your* life. Substitute your problems for Habakkuk's. Tell God you are determined to be joyful and rejoice in spite of all the problems. I believe you will be encouraged.

Listening and Answering

In these days of caller ID and voice mail, people often don't answer their phones until they know who is calling…and whether they want to talk to that person or not. Surprisingly, there's a verse in the Bible about God calling us and not getting an answer. Isaiah 65:12 says: "I called but you did not answer, I spoke but you did not listen." How sad! Almighty God, the Creator of heaven and earth, called the people He loves, but they didn't answer or listen to what He had to say. Basically they hung up on Him!

Has there ever been a time when you heard God's voice speak to you in your heart but you didn't want to listen? So you let His message go to the answering machine, so to speak, and ignored His call? I admit I've done that.

This is so different than the way He deals with our calls. In the very same chapter of Isaiah, God says, "Before they call I will answer; while they are still speaking I will hear" (verse 24). When we call God, He answers even before we call! This means that when you call God, you can be sure you'll get through to Him. David said, "In my distress I called to the LORD; I cried to my God for help. From his temple he heard my voice; my cry came before him, into his ears" (Psalm 18:6). No answering machine and no receptionist fielding the call. Your cry goes directly to God's ears.

The next time you sense God speaking to you, do Him the courtesy of answering.

Grasshopper Faith

The people of Israel stood on the border of the land God had promised them. But before they went in, their leader, Joshua, sent an investigating committee of 12 men to spy out the land. All 12 saw that the land was good and very fertile. All 12 knew God had promised the land to them. But only 2 said, "We should go up and take possession of the land, for we can certainly do it" (Numbers 13:30). The other 10 said, "All the people we saw there are of great size... We seemed like grasshoppers in our own eyes" (verse 33).

My dad used to say, "I don't think any child of God ought to think of himself as a grasshopper. You and I have been redeemed with the precious blood of the Lord Jesus Christ. I believe in humility, but humility doesn't show disrespect for what God has done for you by putting yourself down."

In addition, the 10 spies reported, "The cities are large, with walls up to the sky" (Deuteronomy 1:28). Do you know why they thought that? "Because they were grasshoppers," my dad would say. "Just imagine a grasshopper down at the base of a walled city. He turns his eyes enough to look up at that wall, and it goes up, up, up, up and never stops until it touches the sky. That's a grasshopper's view of a wall."

Are you facing giants and walled cities? How are you looking at them—from a grasshopper's viewpoint or God's? God looks down from heaven and sees the same giants and the same walls, but from His vantage point they don't look very big. And our God is bigger than anything we will ever face.

Celebrate Femininity

H ave you given serious thought to the fact that your being a woman and not a man is God's distinct plan for you? If God needed another man in the world, you would have been one. But God planned for you to be a woman: "'For I know the plans I have for you,' declares the LORD, 'plans to prosper you and not to harm you, plans to give you hope and a future'" (Jeremiah 29:11).

I'm here to encourage you to celebrate your femininity. God gave you a beautiful, curvy body. Pornography has cheated and exploited us as women, but we came from the drawing board of heaven as lovely creations of God. Appreciate your body. Take good care of it with nutrition and exercise. Enjoy pretty clothes and feminine things.

Shortly after we were married, my husband and I visited Paris, France. I'd heard about the prostitutes that walked the streets, but I wasn't prepared to see they were some of the prettiest women there—well-groomed, slender, stylish, and walking with pride. *If they can look like that while making their living in that disgraceful, exploitive way,* I thought,

I can keep myself attractive for my wonderful husband, who is faithful to me and loves me with all his heart.

God looks not on the outward appearance but on the heart. But the rest of the world still has to look at the outside. So enjoy your femininity—not extravagantly or with self-centeredness—with freedom to be all that God created you to be.

Self-discipline

I was taking care of my daughter's four children. Because the oldest was six and the twins were one-year-olds, I needed eyes in the back of my head to keep up with them. While I was upstairs helping three of them get dressed, one of the twins decided he would help me by pouring his own orange juice for breakfast. He managed to open the refrigerator and drag the half-gallon carton of juice from the shelf. I'm sure you've already imagined what happened. As he poured the juice into his cup, the weight shifted in the carton, and soon *all* the juice was on the floor. I can't remember how many times I washed the floor that day trying to get it clean enough that our feet didn't stick.

I've found from personal experience as a mother of three and grandmother of eight that I need self-discipline—and lots of it when everything is hectic. Self-discipline is the difference between exasperation and restraint, between lashing out in impatience and controlling my frustration. But, frankly, for years the very idea of self-discipline turned me off. When I heard the word "self-discipline," I immediately thought of a straitjacket—something forcing me to do something. My focus? "What is the next thing I *must* do?" And I struggled with maintaining the discipline, of sticking to what I needed to do.

Then I discovered that self-discipline, or self-control, is part of the fruit of the Spirit listed in Galatians 5:23. I was so relieved! I wasn't responsible for developing self-discipline. I can no more produce it in my life using my own efforts than I can tie an apple on a tree and expect it to grow. Self-discipline comes from God working in my life!

How do you feel about self-discipline? If you struggle with it, ask God to fill you with His Spirit. As you grow in Him, you'll find self-control becoming more and more a natural part of your life.

Good Things in Heaven

Armin Gesswein was a godly man known for prayer. He led the prayer support for some of Billy Graham's early crusades, and he spent most of his adult life teaching and preaching about prayer and praying. Armin ministered mostly in Norway. In fact, he married a beautiful Norwegian girl whose name was Reidun.

Drinking coffee must be part of the culture in Norway because Armin and Reidun truly enjoyed cups of hot, strong coffee. They're both with the Lord now, but I often exchange emails with their daughters, Carol and Sonja. In one exchange with Carol, I mentioned that it would be great if we could get together for a cup of coffee. Since she lives many miles from where I live, I casually added, "Maybe in heaven? Or do they drink coffee in heaven?"

She wrote back, "Well, my dad sure loved his coffee, and since there's no unhappiness in heaven, there must be coffee in heaven!"

I wish we could peek into heaven and see what it's like. I'm looking forward to that cup of coffee with the Gessweins.

The apostle Paul said, "Our citizenship is in heaven. And we eagerly await a Savior from there, the Lord Jesus Christ" (Philippians 3:20). Peter taught that there's "an inheritance that can never perish, spoil or fade—kept in heaven for you" (1 Peter 1:4). John added, "No longer will there be any curse. The throne of God and of the Lamb will be in the city, and his servants will serve him. They will see his face, and...they will reign for ever and ever" (Revelation 22:3-5). Isn't this exciting?

DARLENE SALA

Forgiving Yourself

The woman wept as she said, "What I have done is so awful! I can accept that God has forgiven me, but I can never forgive myself." Sadly, she was setting herself up for a lifetime of misery.

How can you forgive yourself when you do something you wish you hadn't? First, take a look at God's forgiveness. When you ask for His forgiveness, you may be imagining God saying, "What you did isn't so bad. And besides, I love you so much that I won't hold this sin against you." But that's not true. Sin is bad, and forgiveness was extremely costly. It took the death of Jesus on the cross to pay the penalty for your sin and mine.

My friend Dr. Richard Smith, who counsels people who have forgiveness issues, says that in his experience the people who have problems forgiving themselves don't really understand that God has fully forgiven them.

They don't understand that God no longer looks on them as sinners but as saints—the biblical term for believers forgiven by Jesus Christ. And if that is the way God sees you, what right do you have to see yourself in any other way? In God's eyes, your sin no longer exists. Romans 4:8 says, "Blessed is the man whose sin the Lord will *never count against him.*"

Forgiven sin is blotted out—completely gone. You're wasting your time and energy punishing yourself for it. More than that, you're dishonoring Jesus, who paid for your sin so you could obtain complete forgiveness. So let go! It's time to forget what is behind, as Paul said, and press toward what is ahead (Philippians 3:13).

Have you asked Jesus to be Lord and Savior so your sins are taken care of? If not, why not settle that with God right now?

Small Obediences

As a woman, every day you do many *little* things, don't you? You see that dirty clothes get laundered, groceries are bought, meals get prepared, kids do their homework, dental appointments are made—and the list goes on and on. A woman's life is made up of seemingly endless details.

And details are important. F.B. Meyer once said, "Do not try to do a great thing; you may waste all your time waiting for the opportunity which may never come. But since little things are always claiming your attention, do them…for the glory of God." The apostle Paul would agree with that. He wrote, "And whatever you do, whether in word or deed, do it all in the name of the Lord Jesus" (Colossians 3:17).

I like to think of details as "small obediences." Cardinal John Henry Newman said that taking up the cross of Christ involves the continual practice of small duties that are often distasteful to us.

When I had little children to care for, someone was always needing me. And not for anything important—mostly small details like settling an argument or mopping up a spill. And while that was going on, the phone was ringing and the pasta was boiling over on the stove. There was little time to do anything spiritual, such as extended prayer times or in-depth Bible studies. I was frustrated by this until I finally came to the conclusion that in that particular season of life, the best thing I could do was to meet each demand with the right attitude—doing each task for the Lord with my heart in tune with Him.

Small obediences. As you go about your day, why not dedicate each small task to the Lord?

Who Cut In on You?

Zola Budd became famous in the early 1980s when, as a barefooted teenager, she produced one incredible record-breaking performance after another in women's running. Born in South Africa, she became a British citizen so she could represent Britain in the 3000 meter race in the 1984 Olympics in Los Angeles.

American athlete Mary Decker was the favorite to win the gold, but Budd was also considered a strong contender. The race turned out to be one of the most dramatic of the Los Angeles Games—or for that matter, any modern-day Olympics.

Shortly after the halfway point of the race, Budd and Decker collided. Decker fell over the infield barrier, clutching her right thigh. Budd recovered her balance and continued with the race but finished seventh. Decker was carried off the field by British athlete Richard Slaney (they later married).

Every time I hear that story, it reminds me of the Christians in Galatia. Young in the faith, they were being sidetracked in their spiritual progress over an issue in the church.

The apostle Paul wrote, "You were running a good race. Who cut in on you and kept you from obeying the truth?" (Galatians 5:7).

We're very much like those Galatians. All it takes is for someone to criticize us and we're ready to throw in the towel and quit. I think Paul would say to us, "You were running a good race. Who cut in on you?" No matter who hurt you, it's not a good enough reason to quit. Mary Decker didn't. As Mary Decker Slaney, she went on to set many American running records in 1985. So take heart. Get up, brush yourself off, and keep running.

When God Intervenes

T he three young men were best friends. On a trip to Las Vegas, however, they were involved in a very serious auto accident. Matt and Cole survived, but their friend Steve did not. The experience of losing their best buddy caused Matt and Cole to become bonded as only those who endure tragedy together do.

Matt and Cole enjoyed riding dirt bikes, so eventually they planned another trip—a weekend of riding at an old gold-mining town. Scott, a third friend, would go too. They arrived and were having a great time. Then they were wrapping up the final ride. Matt rode up the hill first and then disappeared from view. Cole followed. Cresting the hill, he saw nothing but a giant hole. He somehow managed to avoid it. Yelling for Scott, Cole then frantically looked for Matt and called his name. No answer. The horror of the situation set in. Their friend had fallen 780 feet into an abandoned, unmarked mineshaft. He died.

"After losing two close friends in tragic accidents, I could feel sorry for myself, blame God, and maybe start drinking," Cole said. "Or I could do something with my life." At the age of 21, Cole made the decision to honor Steve and Matt by living a God-centered life. He travels to churches and schools to share his heart for Christ. Cole said, "I vowed... that no matter how uncomfortable it may be, if I feel the Lord calling me to do something, never again will I let an opportunity pass me by."[57] Cole can now say with Paul, "I have been crucified with Christ and I no longer live, but Christ lives in me" (Galatians 2:20).

When God so clearly intervenes in a person's life, it's for a purpose. Is He speaking to you right now?

Call Me "Father"

One of the most heartrending verses in the entire Bible is Jeremiah 3:19, where God says to His wayward people, "How gladly would I treat you like sons...I thought you would call me 'Father' and not turn away from following me." God, the Supreme Being of the universe, the Creator of all, is yearning for a father–child relationship with His people. He wants you to call Him "Father"!

Many women have trouble thinking of God as their heavenly Father because they had despicable earthly fathers. Rather than loving, cherishing, and encouraging them, their dads abused them, molested them, or simply disappeared from their lives. These women have no concept of what it's like to have a loving father who will protect them and can be depended on.

Hannah Whitall Smith revealed much about God the Father's love:

> Put together all the tenderest love you know of, the deepest you have ever felt and the strongest that has ever been poured out on you; heap on it all the love of

all the loving human hearts in the world; then multiply it by infinity, and you will have a faint glimpse of the love and grace of God![58]

Clearly God wants a relationship with you. His father-heart yearns for you to want to be close to Him. That's what He tells us in His Word! So why not take a moment today to thank Him for being your heavenly Father. He's waiting to hear you call His name.

Forty-seven Kings

We usually think of the Bible as being a book that teaches us principles for living—the divine Handbook for life. But sometimes we forget that this God-inspired book is also an accurate historical record.

For instance, the Old Testament records the names of 47 kings besides those who reigned in Israel and Judah. For almost 2300 years secular scholars refused to recognize these kings as people who actually lived and ruled. Instead, as great as these men were, they were relegated to the status of mythology because no evidence outside the Bible had been discovered that corroborated their existence.

But as archaeologists explored, they found new proof. One by one, each of those 47 kings were verified by a source outside the Bible and so are now universally accepted as real persons. Every single one is recognized as a person who lived and ruled, just as the Bible says.

Aren't you glad that the words God inspired the writers of the Bible to record are true and reliable? That's a wonderful comfort when you're going through difficult times, isn't it? The God who made sure that history was recorded accurately in His Word is the same God who promises in that same book that "the LORD himself goes before you and will be with you; he will never leave you nor forsake you. Do not be afraid; do not be discouraged" (Deuteronomy 31:8).

You can rest on His promises! God said, "I am watching to see that my word is fulfilled" (Jeremiah 1:12).

Remember to Say Thank-you

I came across this poem in the book *My Hope* by Eugene Clark. The poem's author is unknown, but she was a mother who captured a great principle:

My little girl went out the door;
I hugged and squeezed her just once more,
Reminding her as oft before,
"Remember to say thank you."

And then the thought occurred to me,
I'd better check again to see
How long since I on bended knee
Remembered to say thank you.[59]

Pastor Mike Coppersmith tells about a man who was severely depressed. He went to a small neighborhood restaurant for breakfast. He sat hunched over the counter, stirring his coffee. No one in the diner was speaking to anyone else.

In one of the small booths was a young mother with a little girl. They had just been served their food when the little girl broke the silence by saying, "Momma, why don't we say our prayers here?" The waitress interrupted, "Sure, honey, we can pray. Will you say the prayer for us?" Turning to the rest of the people in the restaurant, she instructed, "Let's all bow our heads."

One by one the heads went down. The little girl then folded her hands and said, "God is great, God is good, and we thank Him for our food. Amen."

The entire atmosphere in the restaurant changed. People began to talk with one another. The despondent man said, "All of a sudden my whole frame of mind started to improve. From that little girl's example, I started to thank God for all that I did have and stopped majoring in all that I didn't have. I started to be grateful."

The apostle Paul instructed, "Speak to one another with psalms, hymns and spiritual songs. Sing and make music in your heart to the Lord, always giving thanks to God the Father for everything, in the name of our Lord Jesus Christ" (Ephesians 5:20).

Follow Me

I love the story of one of the conversations Jesus had with Simon Peter. It took place after Jesus was resurrected, when He went to the shores of the Sea of Galilee to see His disciples. Peter and Jesus had some unfinished business. Remember the background? Peter had denied Jesus three times before Jesus was crucified.

So Jesus now turns to Peter and asks, "Simon son of John, do you truly love me?" Peter answers, "Yes, Lord...you know that I love you." Jesus asks this question three times. Three denials and three professions of love. After that, He tells his disciple that he (Peter) will die glorifying God. Then Jesus commands, "Follow me!" (See John 21:15-19.)

We can always count on Peter to ask the questions we probably would if we'd been there and had the nerve. Seeing his fellow disciple John, Peter asks Jesus, "Lord, what about him?" Don't you love Peter's audacity? It's as if he's saying, "Lord, is he going to suffer as much as I have to?" Today we can relate because we often compare ourselves to our fellow Christians, asking, "Why do I have so many more problems than she does?" But listen to Jesus' response:

"If I want him to remain alive until I return, what is that to you? You must follow me."

And through God's Word, Jesus is telling us the same thing. Your experience with God is custom-designed. Your job (and my job) is to follow the Lord wherever He leads you. Thank God for His unique plan for you! Then follow Him one hour or one day at a time. Only He knows how He will use your life to bless others.

Anything and Everything

There's a verse in the Bible that covers anything and everything that will happen to you today. You can find it in the book of Philippians, chapter 4, verse 6. The first part of the verse says, "Don't worry about anything" (TLB). Now, that sounds simple enough to do, but only until something major strikes at the very center of what you care most about—perhaps the business you started, your mate, or one of your children. Then you think about the problem nonstop.

How can God tell you not to worry about anything when what you really care about is falling apart around you? Well, there's more to verse 6: "Instead, pray about everything." Prayer is the antidote for worry. The big question is, "Have you tried it?"

Today, every time that worry pops into your mind, immediately turn it into a prayer for God's help. Our human tendency is to think our worry is either too small to bother God about or too big for us to expect Him to fix. But nothing is too large or too small for God! That's why He tells us to pray about *everything*—yes, every single worry that comes to mind.

The biggest problem most of us have with prayer is giving up too soon. We think that once we have prayed about a problem, that should take care of it. But it doesn't work that way. Remember, we need to pray every time we worry—and that can be pretty often on any given day.

A Special Bible

The following is a true story told by Bill Bright, founder of Campus Crusade for Christ.

In the 1930s, Stalin ordered a purge of all Bibles in the former Soviet Union. Millions of Bibles were confiscated. In Stavropol, Russia, this order was carried out with a vengeance.

A few years ago, a missions team was sent to Stavropol. When the team had difficulties getting Bibles from Moscow, someone mentioned that the Bibles confiscated in Stalin's days had been stored in a warehouse outside of town.

One member finally got up the courage to ask the officials if the Bibles were still there and if they could be distributed to the people again. The answer was a surprising "Yes"!

The team arrived at the warehouse with a truck and a Russian young man hired to help load the Bibles. A hostile, skeptical, agnostic collegian, he had come only for the day's wages. As they were loading the

Bibles, the young man disappeared. Eventually they found him in a corner of the warehouse weeping. He had slipped away hoping to quietly take a Bible. What he'd found shook him to the core.

Inside the Bible he'd grabbed was a handwritten signature—his grandmother's! Out of the many thousands of Bibles in the warehouse, he'd picked up that one! She had no doubt prayed for him, and now this young man's life was being transformed by the very Bible that his grandmother found so dear.

"Oh, the depth of the riches both of the wisdom and knowledge of God! How unsearchable his judgments, and his paths beyond tracing out!" (Romans 11:33).

Volunteers

Every nonprofit organization that touches people and makes a difference in their lives depends on a select group to help make it happen: the volunteers. Oh yes, most organizations also have paid staff, but they would never be able to accomplish what they do if it weren't for hard-working, selfless volunteers who stuff envelopes, make repairs, count donations, and offer to do anything that needs to be done. I know because I've seen them at work at our own organization, Guidelines International Ministries.

I've found two Bible verses about volunteers, and both times the leaders are prompted to praise the Lord for them. Deborah, the leader of Israel, and one of her generals, Barak, were heading up an important battle against Sisera, a Canaanite king who had cruelly oppressed Israel for 20 years. The Israelites couldn't win the battle alone—volunteers made the difference that let them win decisively. After the battle, the two leaders sang a song that started with, "When the princes in Israel take the lead, when the people willingly offer themselves—praise the LORD!" (Judges 5:2). The management of any organization would heartily agree with that sentiment. When people offer to come alongside to help, much can get accomplished. In another verse of the song, Deborah and Barak exclaimed, "My heart is with Israel's princes, with the willing volunteers among the people. Praise the LORD!" (Judges 5:9).

If you volunteer your time to make a difference in the lives of people, "Thank you!" Even if the job you do is behind the scenes, one day your name will be written in neon lights in heaven for everyone to see. And then we will all say, "Praise the Lord!"

An Amazing Woman

All the people of the world—whether Asian, African, or Caucasian—can trace their lineage to this woman who lived during a period when morals sank to an all-time low and the world was filled with violence. This woman is not Eve, but someone who lived at least 10 generations after her. In the Bible she is identified only as "the wife of Noah."

Noah is mentioned more than 50 times in God's Word, including: "Noah was a righteous man, blameless among the people of his time, and he walked with God" (Genesis 6:9).

When God told Noah He was going to destroy the world by a flood, the people of the earth had never even seen rain. For 120 years Noah warned the people around him of God's coming judgment, but no one listened. Can you imagine how hard this probably was for Mrs. Noah? People were probably laughing and making fun of her husband. And when Noah became discouraged from not being listened to, Mrs. Noah surely supported and encouraged him.

And considering the time and place they lived, Mrs. Noah probably worried about their kids because in that decadent age they had no "good" kids to play with. Yet Noah and his wife must have gotten through to their kids because when the world was destroyed, God saved their three sons, along with their wives.

Can you imagine life on the ark? A huge, floating zoo... with the windows closed because of the 40 days and nights of rain. Then there were the 150 days of waiting for dry land to appear so they could get off the boat that was probably messy and smelly by then. And they had to start a new life, building everything from scratch.

When I think of Mrs. Noah, I'm reminded of 1 Corinthians 15:58: "Let nothing move you. Always give yourselves fully to the work of the Lord, because you know that your labor in the Lord is not in vain." You, Mrs. Noah, were an amazing woman!

After You Become
a Christian

Most of us understand we can't earn eternal life. Sinners by nature and by choice, we have no way to become right in God's sight except through faith in Jesus' death and resurrection. But something happens after we become believers. We begin to work very hard toward becoming good Christians. But do you realize it's impossible to be a good Christian by your own efforts?

Paul asked believers a couple of important questions: "I would like to learn just one thing from you: Did you receive the Spirit by observing the law, or by believing what you heard?" (Galatians 3:2). The answer is pretty obvious. By believing the good news of God's grace, we became His children, and His Spirit came to live in us.

Then Paul asks: "Are you so foolish? After beginning with the Spirit, are you now trying to attain your goal by human effort?" Just as we become God's children by the work of His Spirit, so too we mature exactly the same way. We can no more become like the Lord by our own efforts than we can make ourselves grow physically. When you plant a vegetable garden, you water the soil, keep the weeds pulled, and feed the plants to get a harvest. But you can't "make" the vegetables grow. The results come only by cooperating with God in the way He planned for vegetables to develop.

So too we must feed our spiritual lives and keep the weeds pulled that would sap our spiritual strength. But God brings the growth.

So stop trying to be a Super Christian by your own efforts and ask God to take over.

Are You Ready?

James Irwin, one of 12 Americans who walked on the moon, was a committed Christian. He would graciously pose for pictures, including one with our oldest grandson, William.

William has worn glasses since he was a baby. As a toddler he loved his glasses because they helped him see so much better. Every night he wanted those glasses near his bed to put on first thing in the morning. The following conversation took place when William was six years old on a dark evening as he looked out of the car window at the moon.

"Daddy, what's the moon made of?"

"It's made of rocks and dust, William. Astronaut James Irwin went to the moon and walked around on it, and that's how we know. Do you remember that he held you in his arms?"

"No, Daddy, I don't remember."

"He's gone to heaven, and he's with Jesus now," his dad responded.

"Daddy, I don't think I'll recognize him in heaven."

"Oh, yes, William, we'll all be able to recognize each other in heaven. Astronaut Irwin will say, 'Oh, I know you—you were the little boy I held in my arms.'"

"Then from now on I'm going to sleep with my glasses in my hand," responded William, "so I'll be able to recognize him!"

The Bible says one day we whose faith is in Jesus Christ "will be caught up...in the clouds to meet the Lord in the air. And so we will be with the Lord forever" (1 Thessalonians 4:17). Keep in mind that *today* just might be the day we see Christ. Like William, let's be ready at a moment's notice!

Let's Go Shopping

Colossians 3:12-14 tells us that as God's people we need to be attired in suitable outfits. There are seven characteristics we are to "don" so our clothes will be of the highest quality.

The first on the list is "compassion." That's the blouse or shirt because it's worn close to the heart. When our hearts are filled with compassion, we reach out to those around us.

The second is "kindness," and since it's our legs that carry us to do helpful things for others, kindness must be the skirt or pants.

The belt that keeps kindness securely in place is "patience." With patience we have the grace to continue to treat others kindly even when they're unresponsive.

"Humility" certainly must be the shoes—the items closest to the ground. Shoes of humility will take us to those who are less fortunate than we are and need our help.

For accessories, try "gentleness." Not very flashy but oh so attractive. Peter says, "Your beauty should not come from outward adornment...Instead, it should be that of...a gentle and quiet spirit, which is of great worth in God's sight" (1 Peter 3:3-4).

Item number six is "forgiveness." I think that is the hat because forgiveness is first a decision you make mentally, which then transfers into an emotion of the heart.

And how about a coat to keep out the cold? The last characteristic is in Colossians 3:14: "Over all these virtues put on love, which binds them all together in perfect unity" (Colossians 3:14). And love absolutely radiates warmth.

Don't you agree that the person wearing compassion, kindness, humility, gentleness, patience, forgiveness, and love is well dressed for any occasion? Let's go shopping for the wardrobe God picked out!

Mature Prayer

Jesus told a parable about a son who said to his father, "Give me my share of the estate." The father did so. The son then set off for a distant country and squandered all his wealth. Reduced to taking a job feeding pigs, unclean animals to Jews, he was so hungry that even the pigs' slop began to look good to him.

Eventually he came to his senses and said, "How many of my father's hired men have food to spare, and here I am starving to death! I will set out and go back to my father and say to him: Father, I have sinned against heaven and against you. I am no longer worthy to be called your son; make me like one of your hired men." So off the young man went.

While he was still a long way off, his father saw him and ran to him, throwing his arms around him. The dad told the servants, "Quick! Bring the best robe and put it on him. Put a ring on his finger and sandals on his feet. Bring the fattened calf and kill it. Let's have a feast and celebrate. For this son of mine was dead and is alive again; he was lost and is found." (See Luke 15:12-24.)

Beyond the traditional emphases of forgiveness and restoration that are taught around this story is a truth concerning prayer. The young son started out saying, "Father, give me my share of the estate." But his request eventually changed to, "Father, make me like one of your hired men." Immature prayer stops with "Father, give me...[the long list of everything we want]." Mature prayer goes on to say, "Father, make me exactly what You want me to be."

After you've brought all your "give me" requests to God, don't forget the "make me" part.

Hang Up Your Failures

About the time she entered college, Pamela's relationship with her mom became strained. And from that point on things only grew worse. Pamela remembers, "We just kept trying to be close, only to hurt each other again and again."[60] Both mother and daughter genuinely wanted to restore the broken relationship so they decided to take a car trip together to see if they could patch things up.

The tension was pretty bad at first, but while they were having a bite to eat in a restaurant Pamela finally broke the ice and poured out her heart about the things for which she needed forgiveness. To her surprise, her mother responded, "Sweetheart, I forgave you for all of those things years ago. You just didn't take them off of *your* hook and put them on God's."[61]

Don't you love that word picture? Taking your sins off your hook and putting them onto God's. Sometimes we ask God to forgive us for our failures, but we don't let go of them, and we continue to carry guilt for them. But God never intended it that way. Jesus said, "Come to me, all you who are weary and burdened, and I will give you rest" (Matthew 11:28). He meant for you to take the load off your hook and put it on His.

When I was a kid I saw a wall plaque that said "Let go and let God." Will this be the day you do just that? Accept God's forgiveness! Let go of your failure and let God take care of it. Take the load off your hook and put it on His.

10 Things
I Love About You

Wwhen birthdays or Christmas roll around, do you wonder what to give that special person in your life who seems to have everything? My friend Angie suggests an album or scrapbook or even a card entitled "10 Things I Love About You." Although this gift will not cost you much money, it will require time for reflection as you go back through the years of your relationship and choose just 10 things that are extra special to you about that person.

This beautiful gift can be given to your eight-year-old son or your ninety-year-old grandma. It fits all sizes and ages perfectly.

It's strange, but we presume that those we care about already know their strong points. But that's not necessarily true. Sometimes those closest to us have struggled in certain areas and don't realize how successful they've become in conquering their difficulties. Instead of detriments, those areas of their lives are now blessings—and they need you to tell them. First Thessalonians 5:11 says, "Encourage one another and build each other up." There's not one of us who wouldn't benefit from this kind of encouragement. That's why this gift is so special.

And by the way, another plus is that whenever the recipient of your gift hurts you or needs your forgiveness, as eventually happens in every relationship, you can go back and think about those 10 things you love about them. Your anger will soon fade.

Take time to bless the special people in your life with gifts no one else can give.

Florence Nightingale

K nown the world over as the founder of modern nursing, Florence Nightingale was born in 1820 to a wealthy English family. When she was 17, she heard God call her for a special purpose in life. Seven years later she felt that calling was to help the sick and poor by becoming a nurse—in those days a very lowly position that put her in the working class.

When England entered the Crimean War, Florence and a team of 38 nurses went to Turkey and later Crimea to help the wounded soldiers. The military hospitals were filthy and infested with rats and fleas that brought typhus and cholera. Florence, along with countless others, contracted Crimean Fever. She made improvements, however, that helped bring the death rate down from 40 percent to 2 percent, and her work there was the inspiration for the founding of the International Red Cross.

Returning to England following the war, Florence campaigned for improving hospitals so they would become places where lives were saved, not lost. Three years before she died, she received the Order of Merit, the first woman ever to receive it.

Florence once wrote, "If I could give you information of my life it would be to show how a woman of very ordinary ability has been led by God in strange and unaccustomed paths to do in his service what he has done in her. And if I could tell you all, you would see how God has done all, and I nothing. I have worked hard, very hard, that is all; and I have never refused God anything."[62]

"Well done, good and faithful servant!" (Matthew 25:21).

Where's the Piccolo?

The story is told of famous conductor Sir Michael Costa, who was leading a rehearsal with hundreds of instruments and voices. The choir sang at full voice, accompanied by the thundering organ, the roll of drums, and the blare of horns.

In the midst of the din, the piccolo player, far up in a corner, said to himself, "It doesn't matter what I do," and he stopped playing. Suddenly the great conductor flung up his hands and brought the rehearsal to a complete standstill.

"Where is the piccolo?" he cried. His sharp ear had missed it, and the whole piece had been spoiled.[63]

What about you? In life's orchestra your talents may be more in line with the tiny piccolo—seemingly insignificant and hidden. But is it?

The Bible tells of an army commander named Naaman, who was highly regarded—truly a major player in the country of Aram. But he contracted leprosy. Now, his armies had taken captive a young Israeli girl, and she became a servant to Naaman's wife. The young girl was definitely a piccolo player, so to speak—a prisoner, a slave. But she spoke up and said to her mistress, "If only my master would see the prophet [Elisha] who is in Samaria! He would cure him of his leprosy" (2 Kings 5:3). Naaman did just that, and through Elisha, God healed Naaman of the dread disease. God used a simple captive maid to point an important man to Him. From that point on, Naaman said he would worship only the true God.

You do make a difference in this life! Keep playing your piccolo. The Divine Conductor of life's orchestra is listening for your part.

Two Potatoes

The Great Depression hung over America in the 1930s when my dad accepted the pastorate of a small church. His weekly salary was $10.

One day Mr. Smith, a farmer in the church, backed his little white pickup truck into my parents' yard and unloaded a 100-pound sack of potatoes saying, "When these are gone let me know and I'll bring you another sack." My parents thanked him with grateful hearts.

One hundred pounds of potatoes! They felt like millionaires. You can do so many different things with potatoes: boil them, bake them, fry them, stuff them, and more. They really enjoyed those potatoes. But as the weeks went by, the number of potatoes in the sack dwindled. Then my dad remembered that Mr. Smith had said, "When these are done, give me a call and I'll bring you another sack."

My dad said he didn't know whether it was pride or stubbornness, but he simply could not bring himself to ask Mr. Smith for more potatoes. But he did get down on his knees and asked God to tell Mr. Smith that they needed more potatoes.

Do you know in less than two weeks the little white pickup truck stopped at our back door, and Mr. Smith unloaded another 100-pound sack of potatoes? There were exactly two potatoes left in the original sack.

We had a God who loved us enough to even keep track of the number of potatoes in our sack! As the apostle Paul said, "My God will meet all your needs according to his glorious riches in Christ Jesus" (Philippians 4:19).

Superman

Superman began life as a comic book character in June 1938. Pictured as a caped figure of wonder, Superman grew in popularity from comic books to radio programs, newspaper strips, novels, TV programs, movies—and even a Broadway musical. Wearing his familiar costume of red, blue, and yellow with the stylized "S," he has been a hero figure to millions.

In some versions of the story, his arrival on earth hints of a parallel to the birth of Jesus. In one movie version, his father, played by Marlon Brando, tells his son to lead ordinary men to righteousness, saying, "For this reason above all—their capacity for good—I have sent them you, my only son."

There is certainly a hunger in the human heart for somebody bigger than we are. We want someone to look up to, someone who can accomplish incredible feats that we cannot, someone to battle with the evil forces we see furiously at work in the world.

Fortunately, we have Someone who can do exactly that. The Lord God Almighty is His name. Note this Bible verse:

"There is no one like the God of Jeshurun, who rides on the heavens to help you and on the clouds in his majesty" (Deuteronomy 33:26). And who was Jeshurun? Scholars tell us it was a poetic name for the people of Israel, used to express affection. It means "the dear upright people" (see Deuteronomy 32:15; 33:5,26; Isaiah 44:2).

Superman can't be everywhere at once, and there are feats that Superman can't do, but Scripture tells us "nothing is impossible with God" (Luke 1:37). Aren't you glad you know Him?

God Wants
Me to Do What?

W hen you know God wants you to do something, do you immediately say, "Yes, Lord," and then do it? Or do you tend to put it off as long as possible? Let's say that you have a friend who is sick. She *really* is your good friend, but every time you call her, she talks and talks and talks. You know God wants you to call her, but if you do, you'll be on the phone for an hour. Do you begin to make excuses? "I can't call her today. If I do, I won't have enough time to read my Bible this morning." Do you rationalize? "She's probably so sick she doesn't feel like talking to me anyway." Or do you procrastinate? "I'm just too tired. I'll call her first thing tomorrow morning. I really will."

Think about an area where you don't want to obey God. Now, think about it in terms of the devil. He doesn't want you to obey God either, does he? The writer of the book of James says, "Submit yourselves, then, to God. Resist the devil, and he will flee from you" (James 4:7). We often have the mistaken idea that God and the devil are equal in powers.

Not so. Remember, the devil is defeated, sentenced, and waiting for execution. If you believe in Jesus Christ, God lives in you. That gives you the power to effectively resist Satan! And God promises that the devil will flee.

When you don't want to do something you know you should do, stand firm against the devil and submit to God. When you do, you will find the power to do that difficult thing.

SFGTD

Have you received this memo?

This is God. Today I will be handling all of your problems for you. I do not need your help. So, have a nice day.

I love you.

P.S. And, remember: If life happens to deliver a situation to you that you can't handle, do not attempt to resolve it yourself. Kindly put it in the "SFGTD Box" (Something for God to Do Box). All situations will be resolved in My timing, not yours. Once the matter is placed into the box, do not hold on to it by worrying about it. Instead, focus on all the wonderful things that are present in your life now.

Do you have a "Something for God to Do Box"? It's a splendid idea. You can't just stop worrying about a problem close to your heart. You'll be much more effective if you *do* something with your worry. First, tell the Lord about every detail. Then decisively put your worry in the SFGTD Box.

Of course, this box has no lid, so it's very easy to reach inside, take your worry out and—well, worry about it some more. Adopt a "hands off" policy. The prophet Isaiah wrote, "You will keep in perfect peace him whose mind is steadfast, because he trusts in you" (Isaiah 26:3).

To trust God does not imply that you are neglectful. On the contrary, trusting Him means you are choosing His solution. You are simply saying, "I believe You are a good God who wants the very best for me. I am choosing to put the problem in Your hands and leave it there for You to answer in Your time and in Your way."

You may be surprised at the peace that will fill your heart!

The Name of Jesus

Veteran missionary Greg Fisher relates that when he was growing up in the United States, his dad was a street evangelist. Greg was only seven when he went with his dad to a spot in front of Grauman's Chinese Theatre in Hollywood, California. His dad preached to the crowds lined up for the Sunday matinee. One bystander began to yell at his dad—not an uncommon experience for street preachers. But what amazed Greg even at that young age was that what set the man off was the mention of the name of Jesus.

So too in New Testament days when Peter and John brought healing to a lame man. The religious leaders were up in arms. They questioned, "By what power or what name did you do this?" Peter answered unequivocally, "It is by the name of Jesus Christ of Nazareth, whom you crucified but whom God raised from the dead, that this man stands before you healed" (Acts 4:7,10).

Today some say we should not use the name of Jesus in the public arena for fear of offending people who hold to other religions. Yet Greg points out, "It is the name of Jesus that carries real power to transform darkness—the power to heal broken bodies and restore crushed and mutilated souls. Ultimately, what we are announcing is that the name of Jesus has power to save." Greg sums up with this powerful statement: "As a Christian...I can have no other program, no other cure, no other agenda than to announce—from every point possible—that there is salvation in the Mighty Name of Jesus Christ of Nazareth."[64]

Jesus—name above all names.

Women Who
Can't Get Along

When they came to me, the two women were at a heated impasse. They were both Sunday school leaders in a large church. The dilemma was that one of them strongly believed hexagonal-shaped crayons were best for young children to use, while the other insisted that round crayons were the only way to go. As ridiculous as it sounds, neither woman would give in.

A similar thing happened to two women in the Bible. Paul wrote, "I plead with Euodia and I plead with Syntyche to agree with each other in the Lord" (Philippians 4:2). Like the two Sunday school leaders, these women were both energetic workers for the Lord. Scripture tells us many had come to faith in Christ through their efforts. But some difference of opinion had grown into an impasse.

I hate to admit it, but I've observed that this problem seems to happen more often among women than among men. In a board meeting, for instance, two men can argue vehemently about an issue, but when the meeting is over, the two men can go out and play basketball together without holding on to hard feelings. When two women disagree, they don't even want to talk to each other, let alone have lunch.

Yes, it's possible to believe in Christ, work hard for His kingdom, and yet have strong disagreements with others who are committed to the same cause. But there is no excuse for not reconciling. Psalm 133:1 says, "How good and pleasant it is when brothers [and sisters!] live together in unity!" Do you need to iron out your differences with someone today?

He Loves Me

When Elizabeth Prentiss was a teenager back in the 1800s, she became so disgusted with her temper and lack of self-control that she was sure God could never love her. She told a minister friend, "I can't be good two minutes at a time. I do everything I do not want to do and do nothing I try and pray to do."

The minister replied, half to himself, "Poor child...All you say may be true. I dare say it is. But God loves you. He loves you." Then he told her, "Go home and say over and over to yourself, 'I am a wayward, foolish child. But He loves me! I have disobeyed and grieved Him ten thousand times. But He loves me! I have lost faith...I do not love Him; I am even angry with Him! But He loves me!'"[65]

At home Elizabeth knelt down to pray. As she tells it, "All my wasted, childish, wicked life came and stared me in the face. I looked at it and said with tears of joy, 'But He loves me!'"

Absolutely nothing you can do will keep God from loving you. The apostle Paul wrote,

I am convinced that neither death nor life, neither angels nor demons, neither the present nor the future, nor any powers, neither height nor depth, nor anything else in all creation, will be able to separate us from the love of God that is in Christ Jesus our Lord (Romans 8:38-39).

When you are tempted to despair at the long list of your shortcomings, no matter what you have done wrong, friend, don't forget to add, "But He loves me—unconditionally!"

A Green Bottle

A young woman in prison wrote to me and shared the following story.

My life was like a bottle. I always thought I was going to be something special—maybe a vessel used to hold costly medicine or a fine vase. But I ended up just a plain green bottle that was sent down a conveyor belt and filled with cheap wine.

I was packed with other bottles and shipped to a big city, where I sat on a dark, dusty shelf for a long time. One day an old wino pulled me off the shelf and carried me out back into a dark alley. He finished me off, staggered to his feet and, swaying side to side, drew back and heaved me into a brick wall, smashing me to pieces.

For years I lay there.

Then one day someone came toward me—someone who actually kneeled down in that dirty, smelly alley and began sifting through all the broken pieces. How He did it, I don't know, but that Man found all my shattered pieces and one by one He pieced me back together. It's been over two years since He found me in that alley, and He has been polishing away the cracks ever since.

The same Man who sought me out can make you whole. His name is Jesus, and He can piece anyone's life together, like He did for me. The Bible says, "Therefore, if anyone is in Christ, he is a new creation; the old has gone, the new has come!" (2 Corinthians 5:17). Don't stay in your broken condition. Call on Him today and let Him put *your* life together again.

Success or Significance?

It's exciting to think how many people in the world are now thinking about their life purpose since reading Rick Warren's book *The Purpose-Driven Life.* That book has already set an all-time U.S. record for sales of a hardcover nonfiction book, and it is probably being read in most countries of the world. Have you thought about your life in that way? Are *you* pursuing success or significance? Or do you think they're the same thing?

Many people think that to be significant, they have to accomplish something great that will make them famous. Actually, many famous people have never accomplished significance, and conversely, some very significant people are unknown outside the walls of their homes.

Our goal in life should not be to pursue what the world says is valuable but to strive to be what God says is valuable. We should endeavor to take hold of God's purpose for us, not someone else's reason for being. We need to press toward the goal of God's purpose and leave the rest to Him.

In her book *Dear God, It's Me Again!* Gail Ramsey reminds us of the Charlie Brown cartoon where Charlie holds out his hands to Lucy and says, "Look at these hands! These hands may someday build big bridges! These hands might hit home runs! These hands could one day write important books, or heal sick people...or drive a rocket ship to Mars!" Looking at Charlie Brown's hands, Lucy retorted, "They've got jelly on 'em."[66]

Lucy didn't see what Charlie saw. She saw only a mess. Some people who look at you may just see jelly. But don't let that destroy the dream God has put in your heart.

If You Can't Say
Something Nice...

An elderly grandfather who was wealthy but quite deaf decided to buy a hearing aid. A couple weeks after his purchase, he stopped by the store where he purchased the device and told the manager he could now pick up conversations quite easily—even from people in the next room.

"Your relatives must be very happy to know you can hear so much better," the proprietor said as he beamed.

"Oh, I haven't told them yet," the man said and chuckled. "I've been sitting around listening—and you know what? I've changed my will twice!"

The book of James observes, "The tongue is a small part of the body, but it makes great boasts. Consider what a great forest is set on fire by a small spark" (James 3:5). Yes, words are powerful. The psalmist compares them to deadly implements when he notes that men "sharpen their tongues like swords and aim their words like deadly arrows" (Psalm 64:3).

On the other hand, words can bring great comfort and hope. "The tongue of the wise brings healing" says Proverbs 12:18. Did your mother ever tell you, "If you can't say something nice, don't say anything at all"? Well, that is scriptural! Perhaps your mom knew that the Bible says, "When words are many, sin is not absent, but he who holds his tongue is wise" (Proverbs 10:19).

We would do well to start our day with one of David's prayers: "May the words of my mouth and the meditation of my heart be pleasing in your sight, O LORD, my Rock and my Redeemer" (Psalm 19:14).

He Wants Me

Just imagine being able to have anything you want. *Anything*. No limits. You could just "speak it," and it would come into being. That's how it is with God. The God of the universe can create anything He desires. The part about this that amazes me is that He created *us*. Knowing that the free will He gave us would result in our rejecting Him and choosing our own way, He still created the human race. Why did He do it? As incredible as it may be, God created us because He wants to have an intimate relationship with us. He wants to be close to us…to have a positive relationship with us.

There was a tremendous cost to this plan. God would have to redeem us from our fallen or sinful condition so that He—a holy God—could have fellowship with human beings once again. The price was the death of His Son on the cross to pay for our sins. The Bible tells us, "But now he has reconciled you by Christ's physical body through death to present you holy in his sight, without blemish and free from accusation" (Colossians 1:22). What a price for God to pay. What a miracle for us. He did all this because He wants us for Himself.

> But now, this is what the LORD says—
>> he who created you, O Jacob,
>> he who formed you, O Israel:

> "Fear not, for I have redeemed you;
>> I have summoned you by name;
>> you are mine" (Isaiah 43:1).

I am God's! He wants me! In spite of all my imperfections and limitations and "warts," He wants me. What a wonderful, magnificent, amazing, astonishing truth.

At All Times,
in All Places

Author Elizabeth Sherrill was frustrated. Having flown in to speak at a seminar for Christian writers, part of her luggage had not arrived, including her dress shoes. *Of all times for this to happen,* she said to herself. Then a phrase came to her mind: *We should at all times, and in all places, give thanks unto Thee.* "At *all* times," she repeated aloud.

She went ahead with her planned session. At the end of the seminar, several of the writers came up to the platform to talk to her. Suddenly there was the sound of gunfire and breaking glass. A woman shouted, "Lie down, everyone!"

Outside two drunk men were taking potshots at telephone poles. One of the shots had come through a window, and the "bullet," which was actually the tip of an electric screwdriver shot from a homemade gun, lodged in the wall behind the speaker's stand.

As police reports were being filled out, Elizabeth traced the trajectory of the bullet from the window to its resting place, just one inch above her head. Her mind went immediately to a pair of two-and-a-half-inch heels in a missing suitcase and a prayer, "We should at all times, and in all places, give thanks unto Thee, O Lord."[67]

How many times have we come close to death and not even realized it? An auto accident that didn't happen. An armed robbery that God prevented. On an occasion when David had just experienced one of his many close calls with death, he said, "I will extol the LORD at all times; his praise will always be on my lips" (Psalm 34:1). Let's remember to give thanks to our loving God.

God So Loved the World

We were in Vladivostok, where we had just spent some very special time listening to Russian pastors share their hearts about their needs. Each family in that area lived on about $200 a month. Late that evening we went to the airport to catch the night flight to Siberia.

I'd never seen such pushing and shoving! The plane was old, and safety rules were not followed. The biggest problem for me, though, were the Siberian-sized mosquitoes. My husband was good at swatting them, but not before I had some pretty big welts on my arms and neck. I was feeling culture-shocked and thinking, *I never want to come back here.* Then I noticed the music that was playing: "O Sole Mio." William Booth-Clibborn wrote Christian lyrics to this melody in 1921. Some of the Christians words are: "Down from His glory...my God and Savior came." Suddenly I felt so ashamed. What were a few mosquitoes and jetlag and shoving crowds? If the Lord could leave the glories of heaven to come to earth with all its sin and degradation, what right do I have to complain?

Canadian Jonathan Goforth had no intention of

becoming a missionary. But he heard another missionary tell how he was struggling and hadn't had any success in getting someone to help him in what is now called Taiwan. Goforth wrote, "As I listened to these words, I was overwhelmed with shame...There was I, bought with the precious blood of Jesus Christ, daring to dispose of my life as I pleased...From that hour I became a...missionary."[68] Jonathan and his wife served for many years in China.

Let's remember that "God so loved the world that he *gave*" (John 3:16). Shouldn't we follow His example?

When You
Feel Like Hiding

Sometimes I'd like to be invisible. I don't want to hear anyone call my name, or ask me one more question, or expect anything from me. I want to hide somewhere. Do you know this feeling? Do you ever wish you could just stay in bed and pull the covers over your head for the entire day?

Few of us have that luxury. People are depending on us. Husbands and children need our care. We can't risk losing our jobs. So we keep going. There is one place, however, where we *can* go to hide. We can run to God just as a baby chick runs to its mother. Psalm 91:4 tells us: "[The Lord] will cover you with his feathers, and under his wings you will find refuge." For a baby bird, it's a place of closeness to the one who can take care of its needs. For us, being under God's wings means safety, comfort, and provision, as well.

The psalmist David wrote, "I will lie down and sleep in peace, for you alone, O Lord, make me dwell in safety" (Psalm 4:8). God also says through the prophet Isaiah, "As a mother comforts her child, so will I comfort you" (Isaiah

66:13). The apostle Paul wrote, "God is able to make all grace abound to you, so that in all things at all times, having all that you need, you will abound in every good work" (2 Corinthians 9:8).

It may be dark under God's wings, but we know He can see and He will protect us. Run to Him when you feel like hiding.

God Forgets

Mention any date since 1980 to Jill Price, and she can tell you what happened to her: "what time she got up, who[m] she met, what she did, what she ate. In effect, she is a human diary," writes Barry Wigmore.[69] The problem is that Jill can also remember every stupid mistake she ever made as if it had just happened. "It's like a running movie that never stops," she says. "I run my entire life through my head every day and it drives me crazy!"[70]

Can you imagine how painful it would be to remember the intricate details of everything you've ever done wrong? Every night when you crawled into bed, you'd be haunted with thoughts of harsh words you spoke 10 years ago just as if you'd said them today. It would be a nightmare.

Even though you and I don't have Jill Price's amazing ability to remember, we do generally remember for a very long time what we've done wrong. In contrast to us, however, God's memory works differently. Yes, He is all-knowing. But the Bible tells us that when He forgives our sins, at that point He chooses to forget them completely. God says, "I, even I, am he who blots out your transgressions...and remembers your sins no more" (Isaiah 43:25). Those sins can never be held against us for all eternity.

Are you living with a load of guilt because of what you've done in the past? If you have asked God to forgive you, those sins are gone—forgotten by God. So why not let them go too and enjoy His gift of grace today?

The Beans in Our Bin

I'm always amazed when I remember that Jesus said, "Indeed, the very hairs of your head are all numbered" (Luke 12:7). My friend LuAnne learned that hairs aren't the only thing God keeps track of. Recently I received the following urgent prayer request from her:

> My husband, Bill, just came in and was very distraught. We have a grain bin that has $60,000 worth of soybeans in it. He just discovered that it has sprung a leak, and the top layer is rotten. He doesn't know how deep it has gone, but it is bad. The profit from those beans is what we use to put our crops in next year. If we lose them, we will have to stop farming. Tomorrow he will get two men to go into the bin and scoop out the rotten beans.

The next day I received a second email from her:

> Thanks so much for lifting our needs to the Lord. As to the loss, it is several hundred bushels, and

when we sell the rest, they will be discounted.
Now we wait to see what the buyer says.

Within three days I heard from LuAnn again:

Today we took the first load of beans to the market.
They took them at full price. We expected them to
have a little mold on them, but they didn't. That
was a miracle only the Lord could have done. He
not only knows the hairs on our heads, but the
beans in our bin.

Yes, God keeps track of hairs and beans and bank
accounts too. You can trust Him!

Attitude Makes All the Difference

A delightful 92-year-old lady who was legally blind was moving to a nursing home. Her husband of 70 years had recently passed away. As she maneuvered her walker to the elevator, the staff member accompanying her described her tiny room.

"I love it," she stated with the enthusiasm of an eight-year-old who just received a new puppy.

"Mrs. Jones, you haven't even seen the room," the staff member said.

"That doesn't have anything to do with it," she replied. "Happiness is something you decide on ahead of time. Whether I like my room or not doesn't depend on how the furniture is arranged. It's how I arrange my mind. I've already decided to love it. It's a decision I make every morning when I wake up. I have a choice: I can spend the day in bed recounting the difficulty I have with the parts of my body that no longer work or get out of bed and be thankful for the ones that do. Each day is a gift, and as long as my eyes open I'll focus on the new day."

What a beautiful attitude to have! I'm sure we all hope that in the final years of our lives we'll reflect the positive mindset of this dear lady. One of the best things we can do to prepare for those years is to keep in mind that God is our source of hope. The God who has been faithful to us to this point in life will not abandon us in the years to come. The psalmist wrote, "Be strong and take heart, all you who hope in the LORD" (Psalm 31:24). That's God's promise.

God's Gentle Pushes

Our family was traveling some distance by car—my dad driving and my mom was in the passenger seat. Those were the days before seat belts, and I was standing in the front seat between them. I was about four years of age at the time, and I was whistling—a skill I had just learned. My mom had had ear trouble as a child, and any sharp whistle caused pain in her ears. Without saying anything, she gave me a little poke in the side with her elbow.

My dad says I immediately looked over at him and with a grin said, "Daddy, I can read Mama's pushes. That one meant stop whistling." He said they laughed about it, but as we drove, he thought to himself, *Dear Lord, I wish I were as sensitive to Your gentle pushes so that You would not have to deal with me harshly in order for me to know what You want me to do.*

God says in Psalm 32:8, "I will instruct you and teach you in the way you should go." It is possible to have such a sensitive heart that God can impress us with His will without having to put a major roadblock in our path to get our attention. Isaiah says, "Whether you turn to the right or to the left, your ears will hear a voice behind you, saying, 'This is the way; walk in it'" (Isaiah 30:21).

Has God been giving you one of His gentle pushes? If so, you know what He wants you to do, so why not act on it today?

The Shopper's Prayer

Here's a Bible verse I call "The Shopper's Prayer": "Turn my eyes away from worthless things" (Psalm 119:37). How easy to see something attractive and want to buy it. You see it; you want it. Marketers have spent a lot of money to create that desire in us.

But if I want something more than I want God, that becomes idolatry. "Idolatry occurs when one holds any value, idea, or activity higher than God or morality," say Dr. Laura Schlessinger and Rabbi Vogel.[71] That means God is the one who should have the final say in how I spend my money or else I'm making an idol out of "things."

Praying before you shop is a very practical test of whether or not you really need the article. You'll find it hard to pray for something you don't really need. After all, God promises to meet our needs, not our wants, right?

In March 2008, consumers in the United States had a record $957 billion of credit-card and other types of revolving debt outstanding, according to the Federal Reserve.[72] But the United States is not the only place where credit-card debt is amassing. China's Central Bank announced the number of Chinese credit cards almost doubled in the first quarter of 2008, with 105 million now in circulation.[73]

A financial planner once said, "If more people would pay as they go, they might catch up paying for where they've already been." The Bible says, "Let no debt remain outstanding, except the continuing debt to love one another" (Romans 13:8). Yes, Lord, turn my eyes away from worthless things.

Possible or Impossible?

A shoe salesman was sent to a backwoods part of the country to work. When he arrived, he was depressed because everyone went around barefooted. So he emailed his company, "No prospect for sales. People don't wear shoes here." Later another salesman went to the same territory. He too immediately sent an email to the home office. But his read, "Great potential! People don't wear shoes here."[74]

Those difficult circumstances you're dealing with right now—how do you see them? As insurmountable? As an opportunity for God to do the impossible? It's amazing what a difference attitude makes. For years my husband has had a sign in his office that says, "Don't tell me that it can't be done. Tell me how we'll do it." Sometimes what we need to do is simply get our eyes off the difficulties and focus instead on what we *can* do to improve a situation. But most times we need something more.

William Carey, known as the father of foreign missions because of the pioneer missionary work that he did back in the 1700s, once said, "You have not tested the resources of God until you attempt the impossible." I like that because it challenges my faith. Throughout his work in India, Carey faced insurmountable obstacles. In fact, if you want to bolster your own faith, look up his biography some time, and you'll find that he proved by his life that God can do the impossible.

Today when you pray about that out-of-the-question situation you're facing, don't worry that you're asking for too much. Pray big prayers because you have a big God—One who truly does the impossible.

Facing Loneliness
with Courage

In his book *Facing Loneliness*, J. Oswald Sanders tells of visiting Hannah Higgens, a woman who for 69 of her 82 years was in constant pain from a progressive bone disease. As a result of the disease, she lost both arms and legs. For 43 years Hannah lived in one room, but she didn't let her isolation or the fact that she had no arms limit her reach. She had an attachment fixed to the stump of her right arm so she could write with a pen. Using her whole body to form the words, she wrote thousands of letters to people all over the world. The walls of her room were covered with the photographs of people she had ministered to and, in many cases, led to a relationship with God.

"I have so much to be thankful for, so many mercies," Hannah said. "Although I am deprived of health and strength and my limbs, Jesus is far more precious than ever…I can truthfully say that I never feel lonely."[75]

How could Hannah be so isolated and yet not be lonely? She had discovered a secret: the fact that God was with her *every* moment. Most of us know this in theory, but Hannah knew it as an absolute reality. She knew that God meant it when He said, "Be strong and courageous...for the LORD your God...will never leave you nor forsake you" (Deuteronomy 31:6).

Loneliness and sorrow will no doubt come to all of us. You can run away from life or look the facts in the face and meet them with the courage God will give you.

Lives That Tell the Truth

"A saint is someone who makes it easy to believe in Jesus," penned an anonymous writer. Actually all believers who have put their faith in Christ are called "saints" by the Bible. But not all of us attract others to the Lord. That makes me ask, "Does my life tell the truth about God? When people look at me, knowing that I am a child of God, do they see any family resemblance?" It's a penetrating thought, isn't it?

Like it or not, everyone is watching us. Are our lives portraying a true picture of God? The late Ruth Graham, who was the wife of evangelist Billy Graham, recalled a morning when their children were quite young. Billy was out of town, and she had been up with one of the kids about five times in the night. Tired and sleepy, she picked up the baby out of bed and didn't bother to change him—just plunked him down in the high chair. She said she grabbed the closest bathrobe. Her hair and face were both a mess. At the breakfast table, every time Gigi, her eldest, started to say something, Bunny, the youngest daughter, would interrupt. Finally Gigi banged down her fork, pushed back her chair, and said, "Mother, between looking at you, listening to Bunny, and smelling the baby, I'm just not hungry!" After sharing this, Ruth asked a searching question: "Are you taking away someone's appetite for Christ?"[76]

The apostle Paul says, "But thanks be to God, who... through us spreads everywhere the fragrance of the knowledge of [Christ]" (2 Corinthians 2:14). Let's live in such a way that our lives tell the truth about God.

Teach Us to Number Our Days

Among the strangest of websites is one called Deathclock
.com. If you visit that site, you will be greeted with the
message, "Welcome to the Death Clock, the Internet's friendly
reminder that life is slipping away...second by second. The
Death Clock will remind you just how short life is."

If you're curious enough, you can type in your birthdate,
gender, whether you are a smoker or nonsmoker, your weight,
height, and interestingly enough, your general outlook on
life. The Death Clock will then give you a "guestimate" of
your personal day of death, down to how many seconds
you have yet to live. And then the number starts downward
before your eyes. (The date is purely a guess based on life
expectancy tables, of course.)

Why contemplate the shortness of life? Moses prayed,
"Teach us to number our days aright, that we may gain a
heart of wisdom" (Psalm 90:12). I wrote down the esti-
mated date of my death—not because I believe it's accurate,

but as a reminder that each day is a gift from God to be used wisely.

I encourage you to live today fully, appreciating each moment. Anna Lindsay said, "That we are alive today is proof positive that God has something for us to do today."[77] Don't waste precious seconds in bitterness or feeling sorry for yourself. Don't let anger or revenge rob you of even one day. Life is much too priceless for that.

Today God has given you 86,400 seconds. Embrace the day, and with a wise heart, use your time to make a difference.

Encouraging One Another

Sometimes I don't think we fully appreciate how much we encourage one another when we share about the good things God has done in our lives. I, for one, love to get a phone call or an email telling me how God has met a need in a friend's life or answered a prayer. That encourages me to keep on praying until He does the same thing in my life. To the Christians in Rome, Paul talked about being "mutually encouraged by each other's faith" (Romans 1:12).

It's especially good to talk to our families about what the Lord has done. Moses told the people, "Only be careful, and watch yourselves closely so that you do not forget the things your eyes have seen or let them slip from your heart as long as you live. Teach them to your children and to their children after them" (Deuteronomy 4:9).

I guess sometimes we're hesitant to talk about what God has done in our lives because we're afraid people will think we're trying to impress them with how super spiritual we are. Don't let those fears stop you. You know it's a great encouragement in your walk with God when someone shares with you, so don't hesitate to return the favor.

Psalm 126:3 says, "The LORD has done great things for us, and we are filled with joy." Find someone today who needs to be encouraged. Talk about the great goodness of the Lord together. I think you will find that you are "mutually encouraged by each other's faith."

Woman—God's Special Creation

Elaine Boosier says, "When women are depressed, they either eat or go shopping. Men invade another country." We laugh at that, but it's true—men and women are indeed different. God created us that way. The Bible says, "God created man in his own image...male and female he created them" (Genesis 1:27).

A few years ago a historian in England found a book called *Womans Worth* [sic] that dated back to the early 1600s. Its subtitle states that it is "A treatise proveinge by sundrie reasons that woemen do excel men."[78] Whether or not women excel men, as the book claims, science has recently proven what men have believed for a long time—that women are far more complex than men.

A man has an X and a Y chromosome. The Y chromosome determines maleness but little else, scientists say. Men are largely products of one chromosome, the X. But women have two X chromosomes, and the genes in them are highly influential. That means each woman is the product of about twice as many genetic instructions as each man. Researcher Huntington Willard of Duke University said, "Literally every one of the females we looked at had a different genetic story. In essence, there is not one human genome, but two, male and female."[79]

So the Bible is right. Women are different—and more complicated! Yet when men and women understand how different we really are and respect those differences, we understand that each has what the other needs, and we value the unique qualities that each brings to a relationship.

Never forget, dear lady, that you are truly God's special creation!

Your Darkest Hour

When R.A. Torrey was a young man, he had no faith in God or the Bible. His mother, an earnest Christian, pleaded with him to turn to God.

One day he said to her, "I don't want to hear any more about my sins and your prayers; I'm leaving."

His weeping mother responded, "Son, you are going the wrong way, but when you come to the darkest hour of all, if you will earnestly call on your mother's God, and seek Him with all your heart, you will get the help you need."

Torrey went deeper and deeper into sin. At last one night, weary of life, with problems pressing down on him, he decided, "I'll take that gun I have in the drawer and end my life."

But his mother's words came rushing back to him. Convicted by the Holy Spirit, he desperately cried out, "O God of my mother, if there be such a Being, I need help. I need light. If you will give it to me, I will follow you."

With tears running down his face, he put his trust in Christ as his Savior and his dark heart was filled with the light of God's love. He then hurried home to tell his mother that her prayers had been answered.

Reuben A. Torrey became an outstanding evangelist and helped win thousands to Christ. He founded the Bible Institute of Los Angeles—now known as Biola University. Torrey learned the reality of the scripture that says, "This poor man cried, and the LORD heard him, he saved him out of his troubles" (Psalm 34:6). The Lord will meet you in your darkest hour as well!

No More Guilty Feelings

A young woman I'll call "Beth" was listening to *Guidelines' Commentary* on the radio when God reminded her of a shoplifting incident she had committed 13 years before. She knew God wanted her to make restitution. The theft had occurred when Beth went to buy a certain product and discovered she could switch boxes with a less costly item. Over the years, whenever she recalled what she'd done, she felt guilty.

When she went back to the store, however, they wouldn't accept payment because the extra money would throw off their accounting system. So Beth sent a letter, along with a check for what she'd taken, to the general manager of the company, explaining how this had happened during a period in her life when she'd fallen away from her Christian faith. Having asked for forgiveness from the Lord, she wrote that she had a deep-seated conviction that she should make restitution. Now she wanted to clear up the matter.

She received a letter from the company praising her for her honesty and saying that her check would be donated to a charity. Then they added that because her letter was such a wonderful contrast to the usual letters they receive, they intended to frame it. Beth says that she finds it a bit embarrassing to picture her personal confession hanging on an office wall, but if it brings glory to the Lord, it's okay with her!

Beth added, "I am finally at peace."

"The fruit of righteousness will be peace; the effect of righteousness will be quietness and confidence forever" (Isaiah 32:17). No more guilty feelings!

My Will or God's Will?

My oldest grandson was just a toddler when my daughter called him to come to the table for dinner and got an unexpected answer. She was taken aback when she heard him say, "No, Mommy. I'm not going to come. I'm going to play now." As you can well imagine, that day he learned the meaning of the scripture, "Children, obey your parents in everything, for this pleases the Lord" (Colossians 3:20).

When she told me about this, I felt a twinge of guilt. How many times have I said that to God when He spoke to my heart about something He wanted me to do? "No, Lord. I want to do something else right now." You see, there's another power in my life besides God. And it's a strong one. It's my will. And while I hate to admit it, many times my will and God's will are not the same thing. This battle for my own way is the essence of sin. Isaiah wrote, "We all, like sheep, have gone astray, each of us has turned to his own way" (Isaiah 53:6). My way as opposed to God's way. I have the ability to make the choice.

Every day I need to come to the Lord and say, "What do

You want me to do today?" Romans 12:1 tells us to present our bodies as a living sacrifice to the Lord. But as someone once pointed out, the problem with living sacrifices is they keep crawling off the altar. That's why I have to present myself to the Lord *every* day.

So which will it be for you today—God's will or yours?

A Fast from Noise

A friend of mine asked me some questions about the practice of fasting that caused me to dig into my Bible for answers. Although not commanded directly in the Bible, there are many mentions of fasting, including Jesus' instruction about not doing it in such a way that people notice.

Author Terry Teykl recommends a fast that would do many of us a lot of good. It's a fast not from food but from noise. Isn't that an interesting thought? He writes, "Decide to embark on a special kind of fast—giving up unnecessary noise and activity. Say to yourself, 'I will embrace solitude.'"[80]

Sometime today, stop long enough to really listen to what is going on around you. You may hear voices, traffic, a radio or TV, possibly the sounds of machinery running. Every day we're surrounded with unending noise. If you set aside some time for solitude and quiet, however, you will find a fresh awareness of the presence of God. You will also find new strength, for Isaiah writes in chapter 30, verse 15, "In quietness and trust is your strength."

There is, however, a sure way to promote God's absence.

C.S. Lewis wrote, "Avoid silence...Concentrate on money, sex, status, health and (above all) on your grievances. Keep the radio on. Live in a crowd."[81]

Yes, there is a lot in this life that would drown out God's voice. If you're experiencing that problem, consider a fast from noise for even 30 minutes. Use earplugs if you need to. Then listen for the still, small voice of God. First Kings, chapter 19, verse 12, says He sometimes speaks in a quiet whisper.

Cancer

A plaque hanging on a hospital wall puts it well:

Cancer is so limited…
It cannot cripple love.
It cannot shatter hope.
It cannot corrode faith…destroy peace…
    kill friendships.
It cannot suppress memories…silence courage…
    invade the soul.
It cannot steal eternal life.
It cannot conquer the Spirit.

My friend Louise is fighting cancer. Every week she has to have chemotherapy that lasts the entire day and leaves her debilitated. Yes, she gets discouraged from time to time. Numbness in her fingers and toes and the aches and pains that accompany this drastic therapy are certainly draining. Being a person who never has let grass grow under her feet, she finds it hard when she doesn't have the energy to do all the things she wants to do.

Louise has been a believer in Jesus Christ since childhood.

God's Spirit in her life is evidenced by love, hope, faith, peace, friendship, courage, and a conquering spirit. She wastes little time on questions like "Why is this happening to me?" Instead she says,

I know who holds my tomorrows, and I know who holds my hand today! I praise God for the wonderful peace He gives me deep inside and for His wonderful people who walk alongside and encourage me when my body grows tired! While I am walking through the valley of the shadow of death, I know it is just a shadow because the reality of the living Christ is with me, and His joy is my strength.

And then she adds, "I suggest you taste and see how good the Lord really is." (See Psalm 34:8.) Good counsel from someone who speaks from experience.

Woman of Faith

The Bible has a "Hall of Fame." Found in the book of Hebrews, chapter 11, it's a listing of people famous for believing and trusting God. You'd expect to find Abraham and Moses there, but you may be surprised to see a woman listed who was not exactly chairman of the Spiritual Life Committee of her church. In fact, she was a prostitute. Her name is Rahab.

Obviously Rahab didn't get there on the basis of purity—but then, which of us could? Scripture says, "By faith the prostitute Rahab, because she welcomed the spies, was not killed with those who were disobedient" (Hebrews 11:31). Here's the story.

Joshua sent two spies to Jericho to assess the city before attacking. Probably to not arouse suspicion, the men went to Rahab's house. Word leaked to the king, who demanded Rahab hand over the spies. She admitted they had been there but said they'd already fled. Actually, she had hidden them under stalks of flax on her rooftop.

That evening Rahab told the men, "I know the LORD has given this land to you...for the LORD your God is God in

---

heaven above and on the earth below" (Joshua 2:9,11). Then she boldly asked that she and her family be spared when the Israelites attacked—and indeed, that's what happened.

Rahab had a faith that gave her daring courage and earned her a place among the famous who believed God. Psalm 87:4 says, "I will record Rahab...among those who acknowledge me." Now that's quite an honor!

The Weaving

Dr. Ravi Zacharias tells that the most magnificent saris ever made are hand-woven in the city of Varanasi, in his native India. These beautiful dresses—with their golds and silver, reds and blues—are often chosen to bedeck brides all over the nation. Most interesting is that these saris are usually made by just two people. Dr. Zacharias explains:

> A father…sits on a platform and a son…sits two steps down from him. The father has all the spools of silk threads around him. As he begins to pull the threads together, he nods, and the son responds by moving the shuttle from one side to the other. Then the process begins again, with the dad nodding and the son responding. Everything is done with a simple nod from the father. It's a long, tedious process to watch. But if you come back in two or three weeks, you'll see a magnificent pattern emerging.[82]

If only we would let God direct the weaving of our lives in the same way. Only He knows the pattern He wants to create. As Dr. Zacharias says, "We may be moving the

---

shuttle, but the design is in the mind of the Father. The son has no idea what pattern is emerging. He just responds to the father's nod."[83]

You can imagine how frustrated the father would be if his son refused to follow his direction. We do best to leave the direction of our lives to the Lord, who declares, "I am the LORD your God, who teaches you what is best for you, who directs you in the way you should go" (Isaiah 48:17).

Notes

1. Philip Yancey, *Finding God in Unexpected Places* (Manila, Philippines: OMF Lit. Inc., 2000), p. 47.

2. Frances Ridley Havergal, "Take My Life, and Let It Be," 1874.

3. Kay Warren, *Dangerous Surrender* (Grand Rapids, MI: Zondervan, 2007), p. 142.

4. *His Mysterious Ways,* vol. II, Guideposts eds., comp. (Carmel, NY: Guideposts Assoc., Inc., 1991), pp. 12-13.

5. Quoted by Dr. Laura Schlessinger and Rabbi Stewart Vogel, *The Ten Commandments* (New York: Cliff Street Books, 1998), p. 44.

6. Michelle Ocampo-Joaquin, comp. and ed., *Women on the Journey* (Makati City, Philippines: Church Strengthening Ministry, Inc., 2004), p. 173.

7. David Eckman, *Becoming Who God Intended* (Eugene, OR: Harvest House, 2005), p. 153.

8. Lisa Beamer, with Ken Abraham, *Let's Roll* (Wheaton, IL: Tyndale House, 2002), pp. 82-83.

9. Rev. Glenn Burris, Jr., nco@foursquare.org, 2008 E-newsletter, June 2008.

10. Burton Hillis, *Better Homes and Gardens*, n.p.

11. Eugenia Price, *Make Love Your Aim* (Grand Rapids, MI: Zondervan, 1967), p. 97.

12. Del Fehsenfeld III, sr. ed., editorial in *Spirit of Revival*, vol. 39, no. 1 (Buchanan, MI: Life Action Ministries, 2008), p. 4.

13. Sue Augustine, *When Your Past Is Hurting Your Present* (Eugene, OR: Harvest House, 2005), p. 143.

14. H.G.B., "Disappointment—His Appointment," *Our Daily Bread*, Oct. 20, 1972, Grand Rapids, MI.

15. John Edmund Haggai, *My Son Johnny* (Wheaton, IL: Tyndale House, Inc., 1978), p. 80.

16. Pastor Eric Denton, Jackets for Jesus Update e-newsletter 8-13-07, Jackets for Jesus, 5623 Arlington Ave., Riverside, CA, 92504.

17. Dr. Paul Brand and Philip Yancey, *The Gift of Pain* (Manila, Philippines: OMF Lit. Inc., 2000), pp. 306-09.

18. http://www.cowart.info/John's%20Books/Guyon/Guyon.htm.

19. G. Campbell Morgan, *Corinthian Letters of Paul* (Westwood, NJ: Fleming H. Revell Co., 1946), p. 130.

20. John Johnson, Jr., "Great Ball of Fire: X-Rays Spot Mass of Gas 5 Billion Times Larger Than Solar System," *Los Angeles Times,* June 17, 2006, A15.

21. Ray Pritchard, *The Healing Power of Forgiveness* (Eugene, OR: Harvest House, 2005), p. 138.

22. Ibid., p. 129.

23. John Tucker, Pastor, Milford Baptist Church, 3 October 2004, North Shore, Auckland, NZ., http://www.milfordbaptist.co.nz/sermon_20041003.htm.

24. http://www.youtube.com/watch?v=f6pX1phIqug.

25. Tucker, Milford Baptist Church, 3 October 2004.

26. Dale le Vack, *God's Golden Acre* (Oxford, UK and Grand Rapids, MI: Monarch Books, 2005), pp. 244-45.

27. Richard Foster, *Freedom of Simplicity* (Aylesbury, Bucks, UK: Hazell Watson & Viney Ltd., 1981), pp. 114-15.

28. Harry A. Ironside, *Notes on Philippians* (New York: L.B. Printing Co., Inc., 1943), pp. 19-20.

29. Schapera, ed., *Livingstone's African Journal 1853–1856*, 2 vols. (London: Chatto and Windus, 1963), vol. 2, p. 374.

30. I'm indebted to my dad for this selection. These thoughts are from what people tell me was their favorite sermon he preached.

31. Quoted by Elisabeth Elliot, "Gateway to Joy," 11-03-2005, www.backtothe bible.org.

32. Jan Johnson, "What Happens in Solitude?" *Conversations,* vol. 1:2, Fall 2003, Atlanta, GA, p. 68.

33. *God's Little Devotional Book on Prayer* (Tulsa, OK: Honor Books, Inc., 1997), p. 9.

34. Ruth Bell Graham, "I Lay My 'Whys?' Before Your Cross," *Collected Poems,* © 1998 The Ruth Graham Literary Trust. Used by permission. All rights reserved.

35. Morgan, *Corinthian Letters of Paul,* p. 227.

36. Karl Crowe, personal newsletter, New Tribes Mission, April 2000.

37. http://www.truthorfiction.com/rumors/h/hattiemaywiatt.htm.

38. http://www.library.temple.edu/collections/special_collections/hattie.htm.

39. Dr. Margaret E. Brand with Dr. James L. Jost, *Vision for God* (Grand Rapids, MI: Discovery House, 2006), p. 121.

40. Robert Roy Britt, "Name a Star? The Truth About Buying Your Place in Heaven," 15 September 2003, www.space.com/spacewatch/mystery_mon day_030915.html.

41. "Star survey reaches 70 sextillion," July 23, 2003, www.cnn.com/2003/TECH/ space/07/22/stars.survey/.

42. M.R. De Haan, "Small Beginnings," *Our Daily Bread* (Grand Rapids, MI: RBC Ministries), October 27, 1962.

43. John Perry, "Structured Procrastination," http://www.csli.stanford.edu/~john/ procrastination.html, 1995.

44. Wawa B. Ponce, "Putrid Desserts," from Ocampo-Joaquin, *Women on the Journey*, p. 50.

45. Anne Ortlund, *Disciplines of the Beautiful Woman* (Waco, TX: Word, 1977), p. 96.

46. Quoted in Elizabeth George, *A Woman After God's Own Heart* (Eugene, OR: Harvest House, 1997), p. 205.

47. Larry Crabb, "When Life Begins," *Spirit of Revival* magazine, vol. 36, no. 1, pp. 4-6, Life Action Ministries, Buchanan, MI.

48. Jill Briscoe, *The Deep Place Where Nobody Goes* (Grand Rapids, MI: Monarch Books, 2005), p. 13.

49. Joseph M. Stowell, *Following Christ* (Grand Rapids: Zondervan, 1966), n.p.

50. Morgan, *Corinthian Letters of Paul*, p. 209.

51. Ocampo-Joaquin, *Women on the Journey*, p. 127, adapted.

52. Sarah Mahoney, "10 Secrets of a Good, Long Life" *AARP* mag., Jly. and Aug. 2005, p. 66.

53. Mary Southerland, "For Women in Ministry: A balanced life—the impossible dream," www.pastors.com, March 20, 2004.

54. Roy B. Zuck, *The Speaker's Quote Book* (Grand Rapids, MI: Kregel Publications, 1997), p. 83.

55. Frances Ridley Havergal, *Opened Treasures*, William J. Pell, comp. (Neptune, NJ: Loizeaux Brothers, 1962), Feb. 7.

56. Quoted in Mary W. Tileston, *Daily Strength for Daily Need* (Uhrichsville, OH: Barbour, 1990), p. 25.

57. Taken from Cole Hatter's prayer letter, 2005.

58. Hannah Whitall Smith, *God Is Enough* (Grand Rapids, MI: Zondervan, 1986), n.p.

59. Eugene L. Clark, *My Hope* (Lincoln, NE: Back to the Bible Publication, 1979), p. 119.

60. Sonnenmoser, "Road Trip to Forgiveness," *The Gift of Letting Go* (Colorado Springs: Honor Books, 2005), p. 203.

61. Ibid., p. 205.

62. Killy John and Alie Stibbe, *Bursting at the Seams* (Grand Rapids, MI: Monarch Books, 2004), p. 12.

63. Corrie ten Boom, *Not I But Christ* (Nashville: Thomas Nelson Publishers, 1984), p. 135.

64. Greg Fisher, http://africathoughts.blogspot.com, Dec. 1, 2005.

65. Elizabeth Prentiss, *Stepping Heavenward* (Uhrichsville, OH: Barbour Publishing, 2006).

66. Gail Ramsey, *Dear God, It's Me Again!* (New Kensington, PA: Whitaker House, 2004), p. 79.

67. Elizabeth Sherrill, "The Missing Shoe," *His Mysterious Ways*, vol. 2 (Carmel, NY: Guideposts Assoc., Inc., 1991), pp. 46-47.

68. Rosalind Goforth, *Goforth of China* (Whitefish, MT: Kessinger Publishing, 2008).

69. Barry Wigmore, "The woman who can't forget ANYTHING," May 8, 2008, http://www.dailymail.co.uk/news/article-564948/.

70. Ibid.

71. Schlessinger and Vogel, *The Ten Commandments,* p. 59.

72. Andrew Leonard, *The Wall Street Journal,* June 2, 2008, http://www.salon.com/tech/htww/2008/06/02/refinancing_credit_card_debt/.

73. Zhang Fengming, "Number of China's credit card holders doubles in quarter," ShanghaiDaily.com, June 25, 2008.

74. Adapted from D.J.D., "Giant Problems," *Our Daily Bread,* Radio Bible Class, Grand Rapids, MI, Fall 1979.

75. J. Oswald Sanders, *Facing Loneliness* (East Sussex, England: Highland Books, 1988), pp. 54-55.

76. Ruth Bell Graham, "Husbands, Children and God," *Decision* magazine, June 1967, p. 8.

77. Quoted in *Joy and Strength*, Mary Wilder Tileston, ed. (Uhrichsville, OH: Barbour Publishing, 2006).

78. "Women Better Than Men," *Philippine Star*, April 22, 2002, p. 32.

79. "Why Women Are So Complicated," *The Week*, April 8, 2005, p. 23.

80. Terry Teykl, Ph.D., *Lighthouse Devotional* (Sisters, OR: Multnomah Publishers, 2000), p. 220.

81. C.S. Lewis, "The Seeing Eye," in *Christian Reflections*, Walter Hooper, ed. (Grand Rapids, MI: Eerdmans, 1975), pp. 168-69.

82. Dr. Ravi Zacharias with R.S.B. Sawyer, *Walking from East to West* (Grand Rapids, MI: Zondervan, 2006), p. 27.

83. Ibid.

For additional help or comments, you can
write to Darlene Sala:

Guidelines International Ministries
Box G
Laguna Hills, CA 92654

or go to
www.guidelines.org

or email her at
darlene@guidelines.org

--------- **Guidelines International** ---------

Harold and Darlene Sala founded Guidelines International as
a media ministry. Harold is best known for "Guidelines—A
Five Minute Commentary on Living," which is heard week-
days on more that 1000 stations in more than 100 countries.
Darlene writes and produces "Encouraging Words," a two-
minute talk from the heart for radio and other media. Guidelines ministries shares Christ and biblical teachings through
radio, television, video, internet, literature, seminars, and
pastoral training in many countries of the world. You can
visit www.guidelines.org for additional information.